COME AWAY MY BELOVED

FRANCES J. ROBERTS

PROMISE PRESS
An Imprint of Barbour Publishing

ISBN 1-58660-576-3

Published by Promise Press, an imprint of Barbour Publishing, Inc., P.O. Box 719, Uhrichsville, Ohio 44683, www.promisepress.com

Member of the
Evangelical Christian
Publishers Association

Printed in the United States of America.
5 4 3 2 1

COME AWAY MY BELOVED

CONTENTS

This book is
dedicated to the
glory of God
and to all
who desire
a closer
walk with Him.

PREFACE

Come Away, My Beloved was forged in the crucible of life. In the midst of each day's joys and trials has come the ministering Spirit of the Heavenly Father and the Lord Jesus Christ, bringing words of encouragement, hope, comfort, and conviction.

To gain the maximum blessing from this book, read it carefully and prayerfully, a little at a time, searching always for the special treasure of truth for your own need. He who knows you by name and understands your deepest longings will speak to your heart from these pages, shutting out the world around you and bringing you into fellowship with Himself.

Whether you are just beginning your Christian walk or have grown into a fuller stature in Christ, you will be equally challenged and helped. Some books give instruction for Christian living; others inspire to greater devotion. *Come Away, My Beloved* will do both as you open your soul to its living message.

With this book go many prayers that God will enrich every life it touches. Surely we are all bound together in one family in Christ through the bonds of His Holy Spirit.

~FJR

THE CALL OF LOVE

*Jesus said to Simon Peter, "Simon, son of Jonah,
do you love Me more than these?"
He said to Him, "Yes, Lord; You know that I love You."
He said to him, "Feed My lambs."*

JOHN 21:15

THE CALL OF LOVE

O My beloved, abide under the shelter of the lattice for I have betrothed you to Myself, and though you are sometimes indifferent toward Me, My love for you is at all times as a flame of fire. My ardor never cools. My longing for your love and affection is deep and constant.

Tarry not for an opportunity to have more time to be alone with Me. Take it, though you leave the tasks at hand. Nothing will suffer. Things are of less importance than you think. Our time together is like a garden full of flowers, whereas the time you give to things is as a field full of stubble.

I love you, and if you can always, as it were, feel My pulse beat, you will receive insight that will give you sustaining strength. I bore your sins and I wish to carry your burdens. You may take the gift of a light and merry heart, for My love dispels all fear and is a cure for every ill. Lay your head upon My breast and lose yourself in Me. You will experience resurrection life and peace; the joy of the Lord will become your strength; and wells of salvation will be opened within you (see Song of Solomon 2:9–13).

The Need for Greater Faith

*If any of you lacks wisdom, let him ask of God, who gives to all liberally
and without reproach, and it will be given to him.*

JAMES 1:5

O child, do not expect the trials to be lighter than in the past.
Why should you think the tests would be less severe? I test all
things, and there are areas of your life that as yet I have not
touched. Do not look for respite. The days ahead may call for
greater endurance and more robust faith than you ever needed
before. Welcome this, for you must surely know how precious
are the lessons learned through such experiences. Even if you
are unable to fully anticipate them with joy, you can certainly
gain an appropriate appreciation of them in retrospect.

Apply your heart to learn wisdom. This goal transcends
every other aim, and any other good that comes out of a pressure period is an added blessing in excess.

Seek Me above all else.

RESIGNATION

Seek first the kingdom of God and His righteousness,
and all these things shall be added to you.

MATTHEW 6:33

Incline your heart to Me, and attune your ear to My voice. For I would speak to you, and I have an urgent message to give you.

Do not set out to establish your own designs. I have already set in motion My divine will and purpose, and I would not have you interfere. I am jealous of My children: they are Mine, and you shall not intrude in any way to hinder My plans from working out. Yes, you may do many things, but only that which I direct you to do can have My blessing.

Resign all into My hands—your loved ones as well as your own self. Be obedient to the still small voice. Your own imaginings may speak more loudly, but wait upon Me always. You will see the wisdom in this in due time. Fret not about carnal things, but concern yourself first and always with spiritual values. Truly, My promise is still: "Seek *first* the Kingdom of God, and all the other needful things *will be added* to you."

ᚃAITH AND ACTION

According to your faith let it be to you.

MATTHEW 9:29

My promises are of no avail to you except as you apply and appropriate them by faith. In your daily walk, you shall be victorious only to the degree that you trust Me. I can help you only as you ask. I will meet you at every point where you put action alongside your prayers. Only as you *walk* will the waters of adversity be parted before you. Overburdened as the world is with trouble and sickness, I need those who have proved My sufficiency in everyday, personal experience to lead the suffering to the fountains of life. I need those who have found Me as burden-bearer to help bring deliverance to the oppressed.

Never begrudge time given to chronic complainers, but recognize in each encounter the opportunity to speak a word that may lead to their liberation. No case is too hard for Me. Never be taken by surprise when I use you to change a pattern. Do not judge a man by what he appears to be, but see him as what he *can* be if he gives himself unreservedly to Me.

SINCERITY

But without faith it is impossible to please Him,
for he that comes to God must believe that He is,
and that He is a rewarder of those who diligently seek Him.

HEBREWS 11:6

Marvel not that I have said you must be born anew. Of the flesh, nothing that is spiritual can ever be produced. Spiritual life will produce that which is spiritual; and likewise, carnal flesh will produce only more carnality.

This is why I said I loathed your sacrifices. It was not that I despised the ordinance in itself, but I perceived that it was an expression of self-righteousness, showing your indifference to the claim of God upon your heart.

My ordinances are good and holy, but they are to be entered into with deep sincerity and with awareness of their true significance. To sacrifice in carelessness and ignorance is to damage your own soul. Let your spirit never become callous.

Without holiness, no one shall see God. In other words, "Without a tender heart and sensitive, attentive spirit, no one shall see God," for without these, no true holiness will ever be attained.

The fool shall not discern the value and shall cast aside great treasure. The practiced eye knows the true worth of a gem and shall not let it escape him. Thus shall you be in spiritual matters.

Train your eye to discern that which is of true worth, and let it not escape you.

GUIDANCE

The steps of a good man are ordered by the LORD.

PSALM 37:23

My child, hear My voice, and give no heed to the voice of the stranger. My paths are straight, and they are narrow, but you shall have no difficulty in finding them if you watch Me. I am guiding you. You need not look to people for direction. You may learn much by fellowship with the saints, but never allow any to take the role that is rightfully Mine—to direct your steps. As it is written, "The steps of a good man are *ordered by the Lord*"—not by the preacher, not by some Christian worker, but by the Lord.

Trust Me to do it, and give Me the time and the opportunity to do it. Be not hasty, and lean not upon your own intelligence.

Rest in Me. I shall bring to pass My perfect will in your life as you believe and live in faith.

On the Waters of Sorrow

*But as it is written: "Eye has not seen, nor ear heard,
nor have entered into the heart of man the things
which God has prepared for those who love Him."*

1 CORINTHIANS 2:9

O my child, I am coming to you walking on the waters of the sorrows of your life; yes, above the sounds of the storm you shall hear My voice call your name.

You are never alone, for I am at your right hand. Never despair, for I am watching over and caring for you. Be not anxious. What seems to you to be at present a difficult situation is all part of My planning, and I am working out the details of circumstances so that I may bless you and reveal Myself to you in a new way.

As I have opened your eyes to see, so shall I open your ears to hear, and you shall come to know Me even as Moses did, yes, in a face-to-face relationship. For I will remove the veil that separates Me from you, and you will know Me as your dearest Friend and as your truest Comforter.

No darkness will hide the shining of My face, for I shall be to you as a bright star in the night sky. Never let your faith waver. Reach out your hand, and you shall touch the hem of My garment.

SET YOUR COURSE BY MY PROMISES

The Lord is faithful, who will establish you
and guard you from the evil one.

2 THESSALONIANS 3:3

Be not afraid. I will not allow your adversaries to swallow you up. You are My child; I will deliver you, honor you, and be glorified through you. Because of My faithfulness to you, even your enemies will recognize My power. I will keep you in sickness, and in death I will be your sure comfort. I will walk with you through the valley, and you will fear no shadow. Hold to My promises. They are given to you as a chart is given to a ship, and a compass to the hunter. You may set your course and find your way by My promises. They will lead you and guide you in places where there is no trodden path. They will give you direction and wisdom and will open up your own understanding.

Study My Word, the Bible. It abounds with nuggets of courage. It will strengthen you and help you, and even in eternity you will partake of its far-reaching effects.

DEPENDENCE ON GOD

*For we have become partakers of Christ
if we hold the beginning of our confidence steadfast to the end.*

HEBREWS 3:14

My people, heed My words; yes, do not walk carelessly, nor lay out your own paths on which to travel. You cannot know what lies in the distance, nor what adversity you may encounter tomorrow. So walk closely with Me, that you may be able to draw quickly upon My aid. You need Me; and no matter how well-developed your faith is or how mature is your growth in grace, never think for a moment that you need My support any less. The truth is that you need it even more. For I shelter the newborn from many of the trials and tests I permit to confront those who are growing up in spiritual stature. You cannot grow unless I bring into your lives these proving and testing experiences.

So hold more firmly to My hand as you journey on in your Christian walk. Trust not in your own increasing strength, for truly, it is not your strength but rather My strength within you that you feel. You are as vulnerable to the treachery of the enemy and as frail as ever; but your knowledge of Me has deepened, and because of this your trust in Me should come easier.

Move forward with courage and confidence; but always allow Me to walk ahead, and choose the right path.

The Burden-Bearer

He might test you, to do you good in the end.

DEUTERONOMY 8:16

My child, do not share your burdens with all who come to you professing concern. I, Myself, am the great burden-bearer. You need not look to another. I will lead you and guide you in wisdom from above. All things will be as I plan them, if you allow Me the freedom to shape circumstances and lead you to the right decisions.

I am merciful and kind. I love you beyond measure. I intend to do you good; and I will bring to you those who can *truly* help, if you leave all in My hands.

I want you to prosper and be in health. I want you to know Me more intimately. If difficulties come, it is by My order and for your benefit. Others would say you have trouble; I would say you have a test.

SAFETY IN GOD'S WILL

If anyone is a worshiper of God and does His will, He hears him.

JOHN 9:31

My will is not a place, but a condition. Do not ask Me *where* and *when,* but ask Me *how.* You will discover blessing in every place, and any place, if your spirit is in tune with Me. No place or time is more hallowed than another when you are truly in love with Me.

I direct every motion of your life, as the ocean bears a ship. Your will and intelligence may be at the helm, but divine providence and sovereignty are stronger forces. You can trust Me, knowing that any pressure I bring to bear upon your life is initiated by My love, and I will not do even this except as you are willing and desire.

Many a ship has sailed from port to port with no interference from Me, because Strong Will has been at the wheel. Multitudes of pleasure cruises go merrily on their ways, untouched by the power of My hand.

But you have put your life into My keeping, and because you are depending on Me for guidance and direction, I shall give it.

Move on steadily, and know that the waters that carry you are the waters of My love and My kindness, and I will keep you on the right course.

RELEASE YOUR GRIEF

Take My yoke upon you and learn from Me,
for I am gentle and lowly in heart,
and you will find rest for your souls.

MATTHEW 11:29

My child, lean your head upon My bosom. I know well your weariness, and every burden I would lift. Never bury your griefs, but offer them up to Me. You will relieve your soul of much strain if you can lay every care in My hand. Never cling to any trouble, hoping to resolve it yourself, but turn it over to Me. In doing so, you will free Me to work it out.

MINISTERING ANGELS

Be anxious for nothing, but in everything
by prayer and supplication,
with thanksgiving, let your requests be made known to God.

PHILIPPIANS 4:6

O My soul, be anxious for nothing. It is enough that your Father loves you. Loving you, He takes thought of your smallest need. Surely He will not allow you to be put to shame, and He will not be unconcerned when you are in any kind of need.

Always turn to Him before you look to any other source of assistance. It is His love that will light your path, so that you may be guided in finding other help. Surely He has given you ministering angels, who may sometimes come to you in the form of your friends. Accept their help as from God, and your blessing will be doubled. You may also, in turn, be used in similar manner to bless others.

Look not only to the physical for the transmission of spiritual energy. Divine life can flow out to others through your thoughts, the same as through your hands. Use My power, and let it flow out in any form I choose as I direct and guide you. You may multiply your ministry a hundredfold in this way. Be not limited by your present knowledge, but move in and learn more from Me.

WALK ON WITH ME

*Make me walk in the path of Your commandments,
For I delight in it.*

PSALM 119:35

My child, the path of duty is before you. It may look rugged, but it is the only way of divine blessing. Choose some other way, and you shall find only disappointment and frustration of soul. Weariness shall overtake you on the smoothest road, if it is not the pathway of My ordained will. Be not deceived by doubts and be not detained by fears. Move into the center of My purposes for you. You shall find glorious victories are waiting for you, and recompenses far exceeding every sacrifice.

Be obedient: you will bring joy to My heart. Neither the applause nor the scorn of others should be of any consequence to you. My approval is reward enough, and without this, any other satisfaction is not worthy of your pursuit.

Walk on with Me. I will be very near to give you support and encouragement, so you have nothing to warrant your fears. They will vanish as you obey.

THE VINEYARD OF PRAYER

Now He who searches the hearts knows
what the mind of the Spirit is,
because He makes intercession for the saints
according to the will of God.

ROMANS 8:27

O My child, the days are heavy with burdens, burdens that need to be borne upon the shoulders of faithful prayer warriors. Where are those who are willing to make themselves available to the Spirit for this ministry? The planted Word will dry up like carelessly strewn seed if it is not watered with tears of intercession. You cannot in yourself lay this ministry upon your soul, but you can make room in your life for time apart with Me; and as you place yourself at the disposal of the Holy Spirit, He will use you as a channel when the needs arise.

Nothing is more needful at this present hour than prayer that draws its power from full operation under the direction and unction of the Holy Spirit.

I am calling My Spirit-filled believers to concentrated labor in this, the vineyard of prayer. Hidden from human eyes, it is wide open to heaven; and the saints in heaven join with you in this operation of God's love.

Other ministries you must carry on alone, but in this you have a mutual fellowship, for those in heaven have also an intercessory ministry for their brothers and sisters yet on earth.

Rejoice to be granted the privilege of so sacred a task. Count it most precious, and guard against the intrusion of distractions. Nothing of all that you can do for Me is more important in My sight. Cherish it and cultivate it. Live in prayer, and you will know a full life of joy and the remuneration of My blessing!

✛

A YIELDED, BELIEVING VESSEL

But the people who know their God shall be strong,
and carry out great exploits.

DANIEL 11:32

Mine is the wisdom and the honor and the power and the glory and shall be so forever and ever. I make the nations rise and kingdoms fall, but My throne shall be established in Zion and My righteousness throughout all the earth.

I am never defeated, but I am held in abeyance at this present time by human selfishness and willfulness. My justice and My mercy are obstructed by human ignorance and by the lack of faith in even My children.

Be not dismayed nor ill of heart and spirit. Have you not read how I could not do mighty works in their midst because of their unbelief? It is no less true today—and it is not in one place but in many places—yes, even throughout the length and breadth of the land.

Be aware of Me. I can accomplish great things through even one yielded, believing vessel. Remember David, and how I wrought a great victory for the armies of Israel through his courage when all others were paralyzed by fear.

Move on, and never entertain the thought of retreat. Others may actually be going forward on the very path that would be for you a retreat. They are not responsible to give Me the kind of service I ask of you. Keep your eyes on Me, as I have counseled you so many times before.

I have special expeditionary forces, and what if I have called you to join these ranks? Do not look for the company of many others. Much of the way you shall go entirely alone except for My presence.

CHERISH MY WORDS

For You will light my lamp;
The LORD my God will enlighten my darkness.

PSALM 18:28

O My children, obey My words. Do not wander in unbelief and darkness, but let the Scripture shine as a light upon your path. My Word shall be life to you, for My commandments are given for your health and preservation. They will guard you from folly, and guide you away from danger.

Hide My commandments in your heart, and make them the law of your life. Cherish My words, and take not lightly the least of them. I have not given them to bind you, but to bring you into the life of greatest joy and truest liberty.

I have asked you to give, in order that I may bless you more. I have challenged you to pray, so that I may respond and help you. I have asked you to rejoice, in order to keep you from being swallowed up by anxieties. I have asked you to be humble, to protect you from the calamities that fall upon the proud. I have asked you to forgive, in order to make your heart fit to receive My forgiveness. I have asked you not to love the world, for I would have you released from unnecessary entanglements, free to follow Me.

Sanctification is accomplished in no one by accident. Learn

My rules, and put them into practice consistently, if you desire to see progress in the growth of your soul. Holiness is not a feeling—it is the end product of obedience. Purity is not a gift—it is the result of repentance and serious pursuit of God.

☩

Comfort in Affliction

Then they will seek My face;
In their affliction they will earnestly seek Me.

HOSEA 5:15

O My people, has not My hand fashioned for you many signs and wonders? Have I not ministered to you in miraculous ways? How is it you say therefore in your heart, "I will turn again to human strength"? How often have I spoken to you, and never failed to keep My word? Will you not, then, trust Me now in this new emergency, even as you have trusted Me in the past?

Your need is greater this time, and so I have made the testing more acute. I strengthen you in the furnace of affliction, and purify your soul in the fires of pain.

Lean hard upon Me, for I bring you through to new victories, and restoration shall follow what seems now to be a wind of destruction.

Hold fast to My hand, and rest in My love, for of this you may be very certain: My love is unaltered; yes, I have you in My own intensive care. My concern for you is deeper now than when things are normal.

Draw upon the resources of My grace, and so shall you be equipped to communicate peace and confidence to your dear ones. Heaven rejoices when you go through trials with a singing spirit. Your Father's heart is cheered when you endure the test and do not question His mercy.

Be like a beacon light. His own glorious radiance shall shine through you, and Christ Himself will be revealed.

RETURN UNTO ME

Do not be conformed to this world, but be transformed by the renewing of your mind, that you may prove what is that good and acceptable and perfect will of God.

ROMANS 12:2

Return to Me; for I have sought after you, but you have continued on in pursuit of your own ways. I have called to you, but you have disregarded Me. I have placed obstacles in your path, hoping that you would stop and consider and ask of Me, but you have obstinately and determinedly forged on ahead.

Have you learned no wisdom? Have past lessons fled your mind? Are My dealings with you forgotten?

O stubborn and rebellious child, has My love no longer the power to melt your heart? Have My words that you once so treasured become of no value to you?

Put down your anxieties, and trust Me for everything. You need nothing but what I am fully able to supply, with no effort on your part. I do not ask all My children to live in so complete a degree of trust, but I require it of you, because you cannot please Me with anything less.

You are weary, and you should be strong. You are encumbered, and I would have you free. You are hindered by undue concerns, when you should be abounding in joy.

Come back into My perfect will, and finish the task I have assigned you. Anything else is sin. What may be legitimate for another is not so for you.

Come close to Me, and I will minister to you and revive your spirit. So shall you go on, even though the climb is steeper than ever before.

One Day at a Time

Therefore do not worry about tomorrow,
for tomorrow will worry about its own things.
Sufficient for the day
is its own trouble.

MATTHEW 6:34

O My child, have you not known the way of the Lord, and can you not trust Him now? Nothing shall befall you but that which comes from His hand. No one shall set upon you to hurt you, for your God has built around you a wall of fire.

Be content with what each day brings, rejoicing in your God, for surely He shall deliver you. He is the One who has brought you here.

His way is discernable to the eye of faith. His heart is surely your strong tower. In His affection you have security. In His love are your hope and your peace.

Do not question and do not doubt. Each day holds some small joy that shall escape you if you are preoccupied with tomorrow.

Nothing daunts your Father. Nothing can restore the past and nothing can bind the future, but today you may live in the full blessing of the Father's smile. Hold to His words, for they are like a nail driven into solid wood. All else may seem shifting and transitory, but His Word is firm. It is a rock that shall not be moved. It is a firm place to stand.

Do not walk in the path of human reason, and resist the pressures that would project you into conjectures about the future. Live one day at a time! Simply striving to bring joy to your Father's heart is enough to keep you occupied. For you know that He loves you, and you will find your peace as you rest in Him.

The Blessings of the Pure in Heart

Blessed are the pure in heart,
For they shall see God.

MATTHEW 5:8

Is not My heart drawn out toward you to bless you? Have I not said that I would shelter and protect you and be your strong support? Yield your whole being to Me. I am your loving Father. I know your need even before it arises. My provisions are not only sure, but also full and overflowing, so that you may confess with the psalmist, "I shall never want." You will see with a vision denied to many, for your heart is pure, and to the pure of heart is given the promise that they shall see God. How much more glorious than to behold the beauty of a thousand sunsets! How much more thrilling than the sight of the fairest faces ever to grace the earth!

Yes, I shall reveal Myself to you and you shall know Me face-to-face, as Moses did. You shall walk with Me and talk with Me, and I will hold your right hand and be a brother and a friend to you. I shall never leave you, and in the darkness I will be a light for you. Yes, in joy I will be an added comfort, and in sorrow I will be to you the peace that surpasses understanding.

Do not look to people to tell you more about Me. Look to

Me directly, for I will reveal Myself to you in a personal way, in ways no other could tell you. I will be as personal and as dear to you as I was to John, the Beloved. I would take you aside as I did Peter, and talk to you of things that concern yourself alone. I am not only the God of congregations, but the God of the individual, and I am as concerned for you as I was for Abraham or Joseph or David.

You are never one of many to Me. You are precious and dear to My heart, yes, even as a very special treasure. For I love you more than you can ever comprehend, and I long to gather you in My embrace and hold you close to My heart. Do not hold Me at arm's length because you have a sense of unworthiness. Have you not read that the redeemed are brought near by the blood of Christ? Your sins are not covered; they are washed away! They are not only forgiven: they are forgotten! Don't hold back My love.

Be as the prodigal when embraced by his father. Though he would have resisted for a moment, he swiftly accepted his father's forgiveness and reciprocated his love and affection.

I, too, would bring you into My house and spread for you a feast of blessings, and place upon you the garment of praise, the ring of relationship, and the sandals of peace. Come, for all things are prepared for you and nothing shall be denied.

The Healing Power of Joy

You will be sorrowful, but your sorrow will be turned into joy.

JOHN 16:20

Say not within yourself, "Where is God?" for I am within you, yes, even in your heart, and My hand is upon you. You have looked in vain for Me because you have sought to see Me in circumstances and in people, and have said, "I cannot find Him."

O My child, look to Me directly, and rest your heart in Me. Do so with as little distraction as would be easy to do if you were the only human being in the world and therefore would have no one else to look upon and no one else with whom to converse.

Praise Me. This I ask of you in times when it seems indescribably difficult to do so. I ask it of you in love that is stern at this point because I know unequivocally that praise is your only hope for survival.

Distress of soul and grief of heart can only bring on destruction of body. Joy alone is a healer, and you can have it in the darkest hour if you will force your soul to rise to me in worship and adoration. I have not failed you and you have not failed Me. It is only that you have failed yourself—or the disappointment has come on the human plane, not on the divine. Why should you allow any human experience to alter or affect your divine relationship with your Father?

Bring Me your sorrow, and watch for the sunrise of the resurrection. Yes, truly there comes always a resurrection—a morning when hope is reborn and life finds new beginning. Wait for it as tulip bulbs anticipate the spring. The rarest blooms are enhanced by the coldness of winter. The snow plays her part in producing spring's pageant. But when the blossoms break through, we do not then turn back to thoughts of winter, but instead, we look ahead to the full joys of the coming summer.

So you must do also. Your God is your maker. He is your defender. And He is mighty to save. Yes, He is not only mighty to save from sin, but He is mighty to save from despair, from sorrow, from disappointment, from regret, from remorse, from self-castigation, and from the hot, blinding tears of rebellion against fateful circumstances. He can save you from yourself, and He loves you when you find it hard to love yourself.

Let His peace flow in you like a river, carrying away all the poison of painful memories, and bringing to you a fresh, clear stream of pure life and restoring thoughts.

This is not the end. Press on. The goal line is out ahead, and you may yet be a winner in the race of life.

THE DIVINE COMMISSION

And He said unto them, "Go into all the world,
and preach the gospel to every creature."

MARK 16:15

My child, do not chafe at the bit. It is I who have put it in your mouth. I would have led you by My eye, but you have been willful and stubborn. You question My direction because it is not the common way. But I would have you take a path that is quite different from the paths of your friends, and it is because I would bring you into a place in Me and a ministry in which they have no part.

Do not hesitate, and do not falter. Move in and do so quickly, for I say to you, the hour is late. There is great urgency because of the swiftly gathering darkness; yes, this is even the hour of which it is written that none shall be able freely to do My work. It is as when a great storm breaks suddenly and each person is fully bent upon finding his own personal place of safety. Even so it is coming to pass, that in this hour you should be gripped with one consuming purpose—to find the place I have for you.

I have deliberately put thorns in your nest in order to drive you forth. I understand your reluctance, but I shall surely deal with you until you break out of your bondage.

The enemy will hinder you in every way imaginable if you give him any room to stand. Rebuke every detaining circumstance in My name, and keep yourself covered by the blood of Jesus.

Your heart will grow cold unless you keep it close to Mine. Your love shall be turned to indifference unless you keep the cross before your eyes.

The Savior loves the dying world and the lost sinner no less today than He loved them the day He hung on Calvary, bleeding and dying for their redemption. His grace is still as rich and His compassion is still as deep. He has not become weary, nor has He turned His attention to other interests. The preaching of the gospel remains His will, and the salvation of souls is His chief concern. So also should it be yours, and nothing else should be permitted to take precedence over evangelism in your life.

Be diligent. Confess your lack and repent of your negligence. Then shall I give you a fresh anointing and a new commission. I will give you the tongue of an evangelist and will send you to reap precious souls. Jesus, the Christ, shall be your theme, and you will uplift Him, and He will draw the lost to Himself.

The hour is upon you. Do not look back. Go straight forward and allow nothing to detain you or turn you aside. My purposes can only be fulfilled as you give Me your undivided loyalty.

There has never been a day like this. No past experiences can be compared to it. It is as though in history there have been crests in the waves; but that which is ahead is like a tidal wave by comparison!

SACRIFICE, MY STATUS SYMBOL

For whoever desires to save his life will lose it,
but whoever loses his life for My sake and the gospel's will save it.

MARK 8:35

O wicked and perverse generation, have I been so long in your midst and yet you have perceived Me not? Have I not ministered unto you in myriad ways, and you have been blind? Yes, and when I speak to you, you do not hear.

O My children, you go your way as though you belonged to another; yes, you behave not as sons and daughters but as strangers. You hold meetings in My Name, and give honor to men, but not to Me. You boast that you serve Me, but in truth you serve your own ego; for that which you do is calculated to enhance your own position and advance your own prestige, and you give it all a sanctimonious cloak.

"See," you say, "we shall pray," while prayer is farthest from your heart. And who shall hear you? Only your own ears. Prayer is for those whose hearts cry to Me in sincerity. Prayer is for those who earnestly seek Me; not for those with only a pretend piety, who, with selfish and unworthy motives and hearts made fat with self-adulation, are only playing with Me as a child would manipulate a puppet on a string!

Get to the prayer closet! This is the reason I have taught you to pray in secret: because there you are beset by fewer false motives and less temptation. He who does not habitually commune with Me alone is almost sure to find true prayer impossible in public.

You would make Christianity pleasant and acceptable. Your Savior did not find it so. You would make it comfortable and accommodating to your own schedule. He knew nothing of such a false religion.

Lonely nights, He wrestled in prayer, nor spared Himself physical discomfort. Yes, and the more you pamper the flesh as to bodily comfort, the more it will demand of you, until you become its servant, and your physical needs shall be a tyrant unto you in your house.

Do not be deceived. I gave you no such commandment. Hear Me as I repeat to you what I gave to your fathers: "Deny your *self* and *take up your cross* and *follow Me.*" Yes, follow Me, not some worldly form of a backslidden church.

Do not think that it becomes blessed because it bears the name "church." My Church is a living body, not a dead form. My people may be recognized by their humility and sufferings; not by social acceptability and self-advertised success; not by extravagant physical appointments of their structures, but by the grace of God at work in their hearts. Sacrifice is My status symbol, and humanity has not been eager to recognize the type of spiritual leadership I had in servants like the prophet Jeremiah and the apostle Paul.

Do you desire to truly follow Me? Look for the blood-stained prints of My feet. Go, as it were, to the cold, unyielding rock in the Garden of Gethsemane, where self is put aside, and the cup of suffering is accepted. Die to your own treacherous and deceitful heart. Rise with determination to go on unflinchingly, not hoping to spare yourself. Save your life and you will surely lose it. Offer it up to Me, this very day, in renewed consecration to sacrificial living, and I will accept you and you shall know joy as new wine.

ETERNITY AND TIME

. . .a wheel in the middle of a wheel.

EZEKIEL 1:16

Behold, a new day is dawning! Do not let the sound of war and discords to deafen your ears to My message; for I would speak to you a word of encouragement and would bring you tidings of hope.

My little children, I have not gone away never to return; but I will surely come, yes, even at a time when you least expect and when many will have become engrossed in the problems of the hour.

My beloved ones, do not focus on the problems of the world; but look up, for surely your deliverance is near.

My ageless purposes are set in Eternity. Time is like a little wheel set within the big wheel of Eternity. The little wheel turns swiftly and shall one day cease. The big wheel turns not, but goes straightforward. Time is your responsibility—Eternity is Mine! You will move into your place in the big wheel when the little wheel is left behind. See that now you redeem the time, making use of it for the purposes of My eternal kingdom, thus investing it with something of the quality of the big wheel. As you do this, your days will not be part of that which turns and dies, but of that which goes straight forward and becomes one with My great universe.

Fill your days with light and love and testimony. Glorify and honor My Name. Praise and delight yourself in the Lord. So shall eternity inhabit your heart and you will deliver your soul from the bondage of time.

You will experience liberation from the pressures of time and in your own heart you will slow down the little wheel. So will you find a new kind of rest. You will have a foretaste of the Sabbath rest, into which the whole earth will enter before long. When this time comes, I Myself will slow down the little wheel of time, and there will be an adjustment, and it will be as it was in the beginning.

The pressures of time have increased as sin has increased, and all too often My children have been found living more in the little wheel than in the big. This happens whenever the flesh is in ascendancy over the Spirit. Whenever the opposite is true, you have always experienced a fleeting but glorious freedom from the racing little wheel. Is it not true? You have found the Spirit always unhurried, and you have marveled to find how oblivious you had been to the passage of time whenever you have been truly in the Spirit.

You can live here as much as you choose. You can enjoy this rest and disengage yourself from the little wheel as often and as long as you desire. You will lose nothing and gain much. Try it as a therapy for your physical body. It will most certainly be a tremendous source of energy and vitality for your spiritual life!

LIVING WATER

And He said to me, ". . . I am the Alpha and the Omega,
the Beginning and the End.
I will give of the fountain of the water of life freely
to him who thirsts."

REVELATION 21:6

He Has Filled My Cup

Praise Him for His mighty works;

Praise Him for His marvelous grace.

Let all that is within me praise His wonderful Name.

Yes, let my heart be lifted up in thanksgiving,

And let my soul rejoice with song.

For He has delivered me out of the lion's mouth;

He has lifted me out of the pit.

He has put a song in my mouth;

He has put gladness in my heart.

Yes, He is altogether lovely:

More than tongue can express or finite mind can know.

For He has stretched forth His mighty hand

And has smitten the waters:

He has made me to pass through dry-shod. Hallelujah!

For there will be no more sea. (see Revelation 21:1)

There will be no more separation!

He has removed every barrier; He has bridged the gulf.

He has drawn me unto Himself, yes, into Himself.

He has left the enemy in confusion and defeat.

He has led me through the way of the wilderness,

And His hand has been a shade from the burning heat.

Through the barren wasteland, He has filled my cup from
living streams.
He has sustained, He has delivered, He has revealed Himself
In the cloud, in the fire, and in the Shekinah Glory.
Lo, as if this had not been enough,
He brought me to the banks of Jordan. There He did
precede me:
For as the priests went first, bearing the ark,
So He did pass ahead in full possession of all His promises,
And thus He opened my way and
Brought me into the land that flows with milk
and honey. (see Joshua 3:16–17, 4:24)
A land of promise, a land of fulfillment;
A land of conquest, a land of victory.
A land of fullness, a land of abundance;
A land of fatness, a land of unreserved blessing.
Yes, He has been unperturbed, though the inhabitants
Of the land be giants:
For in His sight they be as grasshoppers!
And one with Him shall be mightier than them all.
Yes, and He shall give me Hebron for an inheritance.

Let me not camp in the plain; but give me this mountain.

For though my youth was spent in the wilderness,

Let my strength be renewed:

Let my eyes see with keener vision,

Let my arm be mighty in battle. (see Joshua 4:10–14)

For surely for this hour have you preserved my life.

As sheep You led us through the wilderness,

But now, O God, we stand in the Land;

As sheep no longer, nor You as Shepherd,

But You stand before us as the Mighty Captain

of the Hosts of the Almighty,

And we as men of war. (see Joshua 5:13–15)

We seek no longer

To rest in green pastures and lie beside still waters;

For You have issued Your command to wipe

out the giants,

And to utterly destroy the inhabitants of the land.

Your provisions are full and free and abundant;

But they are not uncontested.

Yes, the enemy seeks by myriad means

To resist our every move toward conquest and possession.

Strengthen Our Faith.

Make us mighty through God for the
        pulling down of strongholds.
    Let us bind on the full armor of God
That we may be able to withstand the attacks
        of the adversary,
    And that we may by the energy of Your Holy Spirit
Deliver to him deathblows. (see Ephesians 6:10–17)
    Suffer us never to fall into his hands.
Fight for us; and in Your grace and mercy,
    Sustain us when we waver. Be ever close at our side,
And forbid that we leave the job unfinished as did Israel of old,
    And thereby suffer untold anguish.

A Perpetual Fountain of Glory

I have fought the good fight, I have finished the race,
I have kept the faith.

2 TIMOTHY 4:7

Write those things I say to you. Write and hold back nothing of all I shall say to you. For I shall speak to you in the darkness and shall make your way a path of light. I will cry to you out of the confusion round about, and you shall hear My voice and shall know that which I do. For My way is hidden from the rebellious, and from the disobedient, and from those who seek to walk in their own wisdom.

But look to Me, and I will be your beacon in the night, and you will not stumble over the hidden things. You will walk in a way of victory though turmoil is on either hand, even as Israel marched through the Red Sea on a path My hand hewed out for them. Yes, it shall be a path of deliverance, and My Spirit shall go with you, and you shall carry the glad tidings of deliverance to people that sit in darkness and captivity.

Tarry not for a convenient time. The movings of the Spirit are never convenient to the interests of the flesh, and I shall engineer your circumstances to conform to My plan and My will. You will glorify Me; for My plan for you excels all other ways, and in the center of My will is a perpetual fountain of glory.

Do not doubt or hesitate, for I the Lord your God go before you. You already have My promise that the work I begin I am able to carry through to completion.

Yes, there is already laid up an exceeding weight of glory for those who go through with Me and determine to seize the prize. For I have wealth beyond your fondest dreams to bestow upon those who have left all to follow Me. All the glittering enticements of this transient life are as chaff in comparison, for God's gifts and calling never waver, and My giving is restricted only by the will and choice of the recipient.

Lord Jesus, I cast myself at Your feet. Let me bathe them in tears, for my feet have been like lead. They have been weighed down with the cares of this life. I have been like one in a dream who seeks to run and is held paralyzed.

Set me free, Omnipotent Lord, and make me Your glad and willing bond slave. Free my feet and make them swift to do Your bidding. Loose my tongue to shout Your praise. Free my heart to love the lost with the great deep compassion of Jesus Christ. Free my affections and nail them to Your cross! Amen.

Ask!

Then the lame shall leap like a deer, And the tongue of the dumb sing.
For waters shall burst forth in the wilderness,
And streams in the desert. The parched ground shall become a pool,
And the thirsty land springs of water.

ISAIAH 35:6—7

Behold, I have placed within you a spring of living water. For My Spirit shall be a continual flowing forth of life from your innermost being. This I have promised to all My children, and this you may experience as you claim it by faith. All My promises are received by faith. None are gained by merit, nor are they awards for human achievements.

It is My Life I am giving you. It is not an emotion; it is not a virtue, though these may subsequently follow. It is Myself. Divine grace, heavenly love, infinite mercy, fathomless peace— all these will spring forth unbeckoned and irrepressible out of the depths within you because My Spirit has taken residence there.

If there is dryness within your soul and you do not have this life flowing forth, you need not grieve or chide yourself for being empty. Fill up the empty place with praise. Through praise you may open to Me the gates to your soul's temple. The King will enter and bring His glory. The Rose of Sharon shall bloom in your heart, and His fragrance will be shed abroad.

For the promise of the Father is to all who believe, yes, to all who are called, even those who are far off (see Acts 2:39). And this promise is the gift of the indwelling presence of My Holy Spirit, promised to all who have been baptized in the name of Jesus Christ, who have repented of their sins and received remission (see Acts 2:38).

Yes, I say to you, it is a *gift*. It is written: "How much more will your heavenly Father *give* the Holy Spirit to those who *ask* Him" (Luke 11:13)! Ask, and you shall receive, and your joy shall be full.

As surely as a door is opened in response to a knock; as surely as that which is lost is found by the one who searches after it; and as surely as one who makes a request receives that for which he has asked; even so, in similar fashion, and with corresponding simplicity, I will *give* to you, My child, the Holy Spirit for no other reason than because you have asked Me to do so. I have not placed this blessing beyond your reach, for it is My desire that you shall have it.

How can My Church be victorious without the dynamic power of the Holy Spirit filling each believer? You thwart My purposes and block My path when you do not avail yourself of this, My provision. Do you suppose I can accomplish My will through a powerless body? For each Christian is to be a channel through which My blessings may flow, and how can you be open to My blessings if you are filled with yourself? Only to the degree that you allow My Spirit to flow in will "self" be driven out.

The open heart shall be filled. The sin confessed shall be forgiven. The hunger after righteousness shall be satisfied. Be as a little child. I will be to you a loving Father. You shall have what you desire because I love you. Let this be your hope, and your faith shall be rewarded. My power is not reserved for a few selected saints. It is available to all, and it is available to *you*. ASK!

RIVERS OF LIVING WATER

The poor and needy seek water, but there is none,
Their tongues fail for thirst.
I, the LORD, will hear them;
I, the God of Israel, will not forsake them.
I will open rivers in desolate heights,
And fountains in the midst of the valleys;
I will make the wilderness a pool of water,
And the dry land springs of water.

ISAIAH 41:17–18

Behold, you are in the hollow of My hand. Yes, in the moment that you lift your voice to cry out to Me, and when you raise your voice to praise and magnify My Name, *then* shall My glory gather you up. Yes, I shall wrap you in the garments of joy, and My presence shall be your great reward.

Lift your eyes to Mine. You shall know without a doubt that I love you. Lift your voice to Me in praise; in this way a fountain shall be opened within you, and you will drink of its refreshing waters.

Pour out your heart to Me. From the deepest recesses of your being, let your love flow forth to Me; let your lips utter My Name.

Let your praises rise in the daytime and in the night. Yes, when you are utterly spent, then shall My speech fall upon you. Then you shall lie down in peace and rise up in joy, and you will partake of a perpetual fountain. As it is written: "Out of his heart will flow rivers of living water" (John 7:38).

Let the Word of God dwell in you richly; for My Words, they are Spirit, and they are Life. They are living and powerful, and you shall wield them in faith effectively against the powers of darkness.

Behold, you are in My embrace. *Rest there.* For My Spirit and My ways are not to be mastered by intellect, but My love is to be received by those who long after Me and who reciprocate in kind. As faith receives the promises, and those who seek after eternal life are recipients of the faith of Jesus Christ (for faith is the gift of God), even so, to those who long for a closer relationship with Me I will give a special portion of My love, so that they may have the power to love Me in return as I have loved them.

I give My Spirit and My love fully, not measured out in portions. I will open My heart to you and take you within, even as in salvation you opened your heart to Me so that I might bring you eternal life. Yes, I will hide you in My heart so you may experience constantly *My* peace and *My* joy. And you will no longer go in and out; but you shall dwell in Me as I have dwelt in you.

Give Me a Drink

Give, and it will be given to you: good measure, pressed down,
shaken together, and running over will be put into your bosom.
For with the same measure that you use, it will be measured back to you.

LUKE 6:38

Behold, the time is short. Do not be entangled in the things of the world, for they are transitory. Do not be overconcerned as to your personal needs, for your Heavenly Father knows what you need, and He will supply. But let your uppermost concern be to carry out My will and purpose for your life, to be sensitive to My guidance, and to keep your ear open toward Heaven.

Miss anything else, but do not miss My voice. Other voices may introduce disharmony, but My voice will always bring peace to your heart and clarity to your thinking. For when you turn to the left or to the right, you will hear My voice behind you saying: This is the way, walk in it.

Yes, I will keep you in the center of My will and My being, lest on the one hand you move into coldness and doubt, or on the other hand you become carried away by fleshly zeal. There is no neutrality in the center. This is not an arbitrary position. For I will fill you with the abundance of My own life.

Your heart will burn with the fire of My love. You shall

rejoice in all kinds of circumstances, because I will share with you My joy; and My joy is completely disassociated from the world and from the people of the world. But I joy in those who joy in Me. My love I pour out to those who pour out their lives to Me.

"Give, and it will be given to you" (Luke 6:38) is a spiritual law that holds true as much between yourself and God as between man and his fellowman. Even more so, for this is a higher plane of operation. Learn it on the highest plane, and it will become simple and automatic at the human level.

And even as I said to the woman at the well (knowing her need of true satisfaction), "Give Me a drink" (John 4:10), so I say to you, Give Me a portion of the love you have—even though it is limited and natural, and I will give you My love in return. Love that is infinite. Love that is abounding. Love that will gush forth from your life to refresh others.

Give Me just a cupful of your limited affection. I long for it. I weep for it as I wept for the love of Jerusalem. I will pour out upon you such love as you have never known. Love that will flood your whole being with such satisfaction as you never dreamed possible to experience except in Heaven. I beg of you, "Give Me a drink." Or in the language of Elijah, "Make me a small cake from it first" (1 Kings 17:13–16) and you will never lack for meal and oil.

$\mathscr{I}$ Will Bring the Victory

Thanks be to God,
who gives us the victory
through our Lord Jesus Christ.

1 CORINTHIANS 15:57

O My child, have I ever failed you? Have I ever turned My back on you, or forsaken you? Have I not been your refuge and your strong defense?

I have protected you and kept you in sickness and in health. Yes, I am with you to help you now. Fear not. My purposes will be fulfilled in spite of your weaknesses, if in your need you rely on My strength.

My will shall be done regardless of the flaws in your life, if you count on the power of My righteousness. I do not work only in cases where there are no obstacles; but I glory in overruling the prevailing circumstances, and I take pleasure in bringing victories in those places where no victory is anywhere in sight.

Count on My coming. Know that whenever faith brings Me on the scene, everything is changed. Darkness is turned to light. Grief is turned to joy. Sickness to health. Poverty to My sufficient supply. Doubt to faith. Anxiety to trust.

No negative force can occupy the same place as My Spirit.

When My Spirit comes in, all these things must go. Yes, they *shall* go!

Ask for the victory. I will come and bring it. *Don't look for the victory—look for Me,* and you will see the victory that I will bring with Me. After I have come, you shall behold the miracles I will do.

CLEANSE THE SANCTUARY

*For My people have committed two evils: They have forsaken Me,
the fountain of living waters, And hewn themselves cisterns—broken
cisterns that can hold no water.*

JEREMIAH 2:13

Wake up from your drowsiness! Rise up and put on your strength, for the night is far spent. The day is at hand.

My people shall be a holy people. But you have gone your own way; you have not considered it nor paused to take inventory. Return to Me, and I will restore you. Put away that which defiles and that which draws your attention away from Me, and I will walk again in your midst as I walked in the midst of My people of old.

Yes, I will walk in your midst in power and glory, and by My hand will be wrought miracles. My power shall be manifested; My Name shall be glorified. For you will walk in newness of heart. With freshness of spirit will you serve Me; for I shall revive you and bless you, and pour out My Spirit upon you, and you will know that it is the Lord who heals you and forgives your transgressions, sets you upon a rock, and establishes your ways.

I have commanded that you love Me with a whole heart, and that you serve Me with *undivided loyalty*. You cannot serve two masters. Purge out the old leaven, therefore, and clean the vessels. *Cleanse the sanctuary,* and bring Me your sacrifices with pure hearts and clean hands. I will not despise the sacrifices of contrite hearts.

I long after you with a love that embraces Eternity. Though you go astray, I will surely draw you back. Though your love grows cold and your heart indifferent, if you will listen, you shall surely hear My voice. When you turn to Me, I shall bridge the gap. Although you have strayed, I have not left you. Wherever you turn to Me in love and confession, I am there in the midst of you.

✛

You Shall Not Be Earthbound

Whoever drinks of the water that I shall give him will never thirst. But the water that I shall give him will become in him a fountain of water springing up into everlasting life.

JOHN 4:14

O My children, what do you need today? Is it comfort? Is it courage? Is it healing? Is it guidance? Behold, I assure you, whatever it is you need, if you will look to Me, I will supply.

I will be to you what the sun is to the flower; what the water of the ocean is to the fish; and what the sky is to the birds. I will give you life, light, and strength. I will surround you and preserve you, so that in Me you may live, move, and have your being, existing in Me when apart from Me you would die. I will be to you as the wide-open skies, in that I will liberate your spirit in such fashion that you will not be earthbound.

You will live in a realm where the things of earth will not be able to impede and obstruct and limit your movement; but you will be freed in Me to a place where your spirit may soar as the eagle, and you may make your nest in a place of safety and solitude, unmolested and undefiled by the sordidness of the world.

You will have companionship but it will be the companionship of those like-minded with you; yes, those who like yourself are done with the beggarly elements, and whose sense of values has been readjusted so that they deem the unseen as of greater worth than the seen, and the spiritual riches more precious than the wealth of the world.

Be done with petty things. Be done with small dreams. Give Me all that you have and are; and I will share with you abundantly all that I have and all that I am.

Be to Me a reservoir where I can store up My reserve of strength and power and blessing, and so make it readily available to the thirsty. Never be caught like the man in the biblical account who, having unexpected guests at midnight, had nothing to set before them (see Luke 11:6).

Take from Me largely, that you will never be holding an empty cup when the thirsty ask you for a drink, and never be lacking when the sick ask for bread. For if you have but a little, I will multiply it; but if you have nothing, you will be ashamed.

Receive My love freely. Drink of My Spirit—yes, drink deeply, so that it will be truly *waters to swim in* (see Ezekiel 47:5). And move out by faith to the realms of the manifestations of My power, yes, mount up on the wings of My power. For there are powers of the air to be subdued and conquered. You need faith and the liberty and power of the Holy Spirit to overcome these and rise above them.

For My Church shall be an overcoming church, and My Bride shall be a heavenly being. I will not choose Me a wife out of Egypt. I will take to Me one who has chosen to make My home her home and My people her people, even as Ruth did. But she who turns back will be like Orpah or even like Lot's wife. She shall not enter into My inheritance.

You Cannot Weary My Love

He said to Thomas, "Reach your finger here, and look at My hands;
and reach your hand here, and put it into My side.
Do not be unbelieving, but believing."

JOHN 20:27

Lift your eyes, and look upon Me. For though you have for-gotten Me, I have not forgotten you. While you have busied yourselves with your daily occupations, *I have still been occupied with you.* When your mind has been captured by the affairs of life, *My thoughts have been of you.*

My little children, you cannot weary My love. You may grieve My heart, but My love is changeless, infinite. I long for you to turn to Me. My hands are full of blessings that I desire to give you. I long to hear your voice. You speak much with others—O speak to Me! I have so much to tell you.

I am not a remote power. I am an intimate person, even as yourself. Have you forgotten that I made you in My own image and likeness? It is not that *I am as you, but you are like Me.* Do not let material and physical elements destroy your comprehension of Me as a *person.*

"Touch Me and handle Me," I told Thomas (see John 20:27). To you I say: Cast yourself upon Me; pour your love out to Me. *You will discover that I am as tangible to you as I was to Thomas.* Reach forth your hand, and lay it upon My broken heart. Yes, take hold of My nail-pierced hand. Now, can you still doubt My love?

+‡+

COURAGE

And take the helmet of salvation, and the sword of the Spirit, which is the word of God.

EPHESIANS 6:17

My people shall not go mourning, for I the Lord will be their rejoicing and their song. They will not be a complaining people, for I will take away the murmuring from your streets. Will I lead into the battlefronts an army of weeping women? Will I ask the fainthearted to war?

No, but I shall give My people brave and courageous spirits, and I will make them strong of heart. I will give them the spirit of the martyrs, for they will be My witnesses of resurrection power. They shall be stalwart. They shall be steadfast. And I will remove from the ranks those who are timid and those who desire comfort and security. My way is a way of sacrifice, and the rewards are not in worldly honors.

So take upon you the full armor of God: the helmet of

salvation, the breastplate of righteousness, the loins girded with truth, feet shod with the preparation of the gospel of peace, having the shield of faith and the sword of the Spirit.

Yes, My people, this is a hand-to-hand combat. You shall stand against the foe face-to-face. You will not turn in retreat lest you be slain; for there is no armor to protect the back. The coward will perish.

You have not wrestled in any measure such as He, the Lord Jesus. You are not prepared to enter into this conflict as long as you are absorbed in the luxuries and the personal comforts of normal life. For every soldier must give first place to his obligation to the armed forces, and second place to his own private life and wishes. Even so you must do, if you would be My followers. Even so did Jesus during His earthly ministry. His entire life was subordinated to the Father's will.

As it is written, "Even Christ did not please Himself" (Romans 15:3). How dare you risk allowing the flesh to manifest its desires? They can be only evil continually. No good thing can come out of a deceitful heart. As the old hymn says, "The arm of flesh will fail you—you dare not trust your own."

Only that which is generated within you by the Spirit of God can bring forth righteousness; do not be conformed to this world, but be transformed by the renewing of your mind, that you may personally discover what is the good and acceptable and perfect will of God.

The Sense of Perspective

Most assuredly, I say to you, he who hears My word and believes in Him
who sent Me has everlasting life, and shall not come into judgment,
but has passed from death into life.

JOHN 5:24

O My little ones, how precious you are to Me—yes, you are the apple of My eye, I will guard you from harm. Never let the fears that are common to the world creep into your hearts, for you are not of the world, My children, and you need not fear the things that plague the minds of the ungodly.

You need not fear the coming judgment, for if your sins have been confessed and forgiven and cleansed by the blood of Jesus, you will not be condemned, because you are already passed from death into eternal life. You need not fear the Day of Judgment. It is sent to try the world, and you are not of the world, My little children. Indeed, it is you who will help Me in judging the world (see 1 Corinthians 6:3).

Who knows the crimes of the world better than My children? Haven't many crimes been perpetrated against you, even while you sought to serve and worship Me? Indeed, mankind resists My hand upon them. But how can they punish Me? They can most naturally express their hostility toward the Almighty and show their resentment against My laws by mistreating My children. Will you not be called to testify against them?

This is not incompatible with the law of forgiveness that now binds you, for the Scriptures say to love your enemies and treat those who do you wrong with kindness. It is the same with you as with Me. Today is the day of My grace, and it operates through you also, bringing loving forgiveness to all, even the spirit manifest by Jesus as He hung on the cross. But the Day of Judgment shall be a day of strict reckoning, and it shall be a day of wrath against both sin and sinner. It is inescapable, for it is appointed for men to die once, but after this is the judgment.

Do you fear calamity? You are only human if you do. But have you considered My servant, the apostle Paul? In shipwrecks, in adversities, in distresses, in physical privations, in persecutions and threat of death by wild beasts; in all of these, he rejoiced in his God. He was more than victorious. He was given a supernatural joy in the midst of all his distress. You may have it too.

Have you read the testimony of My servant Habakkuk? And have you read of the latter days of My servant Job? There can be no permanent loss in the life of My children, for out of the seeds of every calamity rises a whole crop of new victories. It is the way I have made it. The greatest evidence of this truth is Calvary. By design of man, out of the cruelty of wicked hearts, Christ was made a martyr. But by the Hand of a greater power, He was made to become a Savior—even the Savior of the very men who put Him to death.

No, My children, do not fear. Remember the words of Holy Scripture: "Do not fear, little flock, for it is your Father's good pleasure to give you the kingdom" (Luke 12:32). Here you have it again—I am not simply preserving you, but I am doing so for the purpose of sharing with you My kingdom power. If you can catch the vision of what the days ahead hold in store for you in My great kingdom, you will gain a whole new perspective, so that as you view the present, transient scene, its true dimension will come into focus in proportion to the whole panoramic picture.

I can give you this sense of perspective, because I see the whole scroll of the ages as though it were already unrolled before Me—so that the future is as clearly in view as the past. Look over My shoulder! Look at your own life from My vantage point. My Spirit will bring you revelation and understanding, light and wisdom.

The person of mature years has gained wisdom by experience. You may gain wisdom (if you desire it) by drawing on My experience. I am infinite and eternal, and though you may be unable to grasp it, I have experienced both what you know as the past and what you refer to as the future.

You live within the confines of time. I live outside all such bounds and limitations.

Do not be disturbed by your ignorance. Seek diligently after My wisdom. It will greatly enrich your life. Have I not commanded you to do so?

It will bring you more tranquility than any other spiritual pursuit. It will bring you greater poise and sense of values than you would ever be able to gain otherwise. For you must profit either by your own experience or by My experience. What a contrast exists between the two!

Seek My wisdom, and make it the guide of your life. Let the winds blow and storms beat. Your house shall stand.

REMOVE THE ROCKS

How can you say. . . . "Brother, let me remove the speck that is in your eye," when you yourself do not see the plank that is in your own eye?

LUKE 6:42

O My people, I have called you to repentance and confession and forgiveness and cleansing; but you have listened to My words as though they were but slight rustlings in the treetops— as though they were of little consequence and could be brushed aside at will. Behold, I say to you: You cannot resist My Spirit without suffering pain; and you cannot turn a deaf ear to My words without falling into the snare of the enemy.

You have not cried to Me with all your hearts, but you have complained that I have not heard your prayers. As it is written: "He [the Lord] is a rewarder of those who *diligently* seek Him" (Hebrews 11:6). And again: *"You will seek Me and find Me, when you search for Me with ALL your heart"* (Jeremiah 29:13).

Look no more to My hand to supply freely your needs when you have not humbled your hearts and cleansed your hands and come to Me with the sacrifice I have required—even a broken and a contrite heart. You need not expect Me to speak to you when your ears are heavy from listening to evil reports.

Just as there can come no healing to the physical body until first the poison is removed from the system, so there can come no blessing and revival and renewal to My Body, the Church, until evil is put away and sins are purged. Your eyes will not look upon My face while they are still engaged in viewing the faults and imperfections in the brethren. When you look to Me in truth and sincerity and repentance, you shall indeed see Me, and having seen Me, you will look upon your brothers and sisters with love and understanding and patience, knowing full well the needs in your own heart and life.

Behold, after the weeds are cleared; after the fallow ground is broken up; yes, after the rocks have been removed: *then I will send the showers,* and then I will minister to your hearts in kindness and in blessing. Although My heart has been grieved, I love you; and though I have hidden My face from you for a time, in great tenderness I will gather you again unto Myself.

I will withhold My chastening rod when you turn to Me in repentance. If you confess your sins and recognize your transgressions, I will be faithful to you and forgive you. I will cleanse and restore you. You will find peace. You will say the tears of godly sorrow have been sweet.

The heart that grieves over sin shall experience genuine comfort. There is nothing like it in any of the comforts of the world. If you bathe My feet in your tears, I shall clasp you to My heart in love. I cannot describe to you My love. I can only give it to you. It is beyond the Cross. Go through. The Spirit alone can communicate what lies on the other side.

PUT AWAY THE IDOLS

They complained against the landowner, saying,
"These last men have worked only one hour,
and you made them equal to us who
have borne the burden
and the heat of the day."
But he answered one of them and said,
"Friend, I am doing you no wrong. . . .
I wish to give to this last man
the same as to you."

MATTHEW 20:11–14

Behold, I have put My Spirit upon you that you should cry and not keep silent. Yes, I have spoken to you that you might know the burden of the Lord, and might understand what is in My heart.

For I love My people, My chosen and elect; and My heart grieves over them, because they are turned aside. They have known My love; yes, they have tasted of My goodness and entered into My grace, and I have given them My salvation; but their love has grown cold, their desires have turned to others, and their ways are the paths of self-seeking and folly.

For I am a jealous God, and I will not share My glory with another. Yes, I will pour out My goodness without restraint upon every open heart; and to all who cry out to Me, I will be gracious.

But My people have not cried; they have not called. They have been satisfied with the husks of this present world, and in an hour of indifference, they have allowed the pleasures of this life to fill that place which belongs only to Me. Yes, it has displaced My Spirit, but it does not satisfy.

O that they might return to Me, for as the father awaited the return of the prodigal, so I long for My people. My heart is lifted up with grief, and My tears flow as a fountain. For I love them. My soul is drawn out to them.

Return to Me, and I will return to you. *Put away the idols,* and give Me your heart. Lay your heart open before Me, and I will purge away the dross. I will cleanse it and fill it with My glory. You will no longer crave the leeks and the garlic of Egypt. You will no longer feed upon chaff; but I will satisfy your soul with manna from heaven, and with milk and honey you shall be nourished.

And your health will return to you, and your vigor, and you will serve Me with fresh energy. You shall go forth in new power, and My joy shall be your constant portion. Though you labor in the last hour before sunset, you shall be rewarded the same as those who preceded you (see Matthew 20:1–16).

Saturate Your Soul in the Oil of the Spirit

We are hard pressed on every side, yet not crushed; we are perplexed,
but not in despair; persecuted, but not forsaken.

2 CORINTHIANS 4:8–9

Through My people the eternal glory of the Father shall be manifested unto the nations. For the everlasting power of the Godhead is incarnate in My chosen ones. Is it not written that the kingdom of God dwells within you? In the day that you make Me Lord in your life and give Me the scepter and allow Me to reign within, then I will begin to move, and My power will radiate from your entire being. Then I will bring to pass miracles—when you walk in uprightness and with mercy toward your acquaintances and even toward your enemies.

Do not imagine for a moment that I can do any mighty works in the atmosphere of hostility, evil, and rebellion. Come to Me with a clean heart and a right spirit, in sincerity, in honesty. If you desire Me to work in your midst, do not be devious in your ways or indirect in your dealings with others (see 2 Corinthians 4:2). It is the pure in heart who see God. It is those who seek after a holy walk and who set their heart toward holy living who inherit the promises and who come into My holy hill.

Know that in heaven nothing enters that can taint or mar. The beauty of the living God dwells there. Where there is holiness, there is beauty. Where there are beauty and holiness, there is omnipotence. Where there is the activity of the Almighty, there are forces of Life continually working to produce within you a measure of the life, health, and strength that are in Him.

Why will you tolerate any idea of discouragement? Nothing can ever be accomplished for good in this frame of mind. Sin brings forth death; and any negative current flowing within your body will produce a steady regression.

I will prepare within you a different attitude of mind. Thoughts that have been in confusion, I will reorganize. I will not bring to bear upon you pressures that will weaken you. I will be the strength you need. I will be the inner fortification that will bear you up even in the time of strain and crisis.

SATURATE YOUR SOUL IN THE OIL OF THE HOLY SPIRIT, *and keep your channel of communication always open to your Heavenly Father*. His desire is toward you, and He will be your strong habitation.

THE ECONOMY
OF THE KINGDOM

*For with the same measure that you use,
it will be measured back to you.*

LUKE 6:38

Bring Me all the tithes, and I will open the gates of heaven and pour down upon you a fourfold blessing. Yes, I will bless you in the grace of giving, and I will bless you with joy. You shall open the door of ministry for My servants, and you shall partake of the fruits that will come as a result.

You will never give to Me and become the poorer for it. In exchange for your small gifts, you shall be given My boundless riches. Through the contribution that comes from a willing heart, I will be freed to bestow the abundance of heaven, treasures you could never purchase from the world.

But see that you give joyfully—for God delights in a cheerful giver—otherwise you grieve the Spirit, for has He not given to you without measure? As you have received freely (for God always has a generous heart), you are required to give without grudging, not mindful of any sacrifice.

Your giving seems sacrificial only when viewed in the light of what other use you could have made of the money. Give freely to the work of My Kingdom, and I will add to you the things you need.

Be My agents of righteousness and goodwill, and I will prove Myself to you as your loving Heavenly Father, supplying your needs out of the riches of My own treasury—and this, too, will be an exciting adventure in your walk in the Spirit.

Indeed, you shall see in what miraculous ways I will care for your needs, and even in the process of doing this I will further the Kingdom; for others who give to you will also receive spiritual blessings.

Yes, My child, My economy is wonderful! My Kingdom truly is not the kingdom of the world. Even the material gifts you dedicate to Me immediately become "spiritual currency." You have given to Me that which I can multiply in spiritual blessings to you and to others.

Give, My children. Your poverty shall be turned to wealth, and you will be freed from your anxieties concerning financial matters. Give, and it will be given to you: good measure, pressed down, shaken together, and running over will be put into your bosom.

HOUSEHOLD SALVATION

I will sing of the mercies of the LORD forever;
With my mouth will I make known Your faithfulness to all generations.

PSALM 89:1

O My child, I have loved you with an everlasting love, and with strong cords I have bound you to Myself. In the day of adversity I have been your refuge, and in the hour of need I have held you up, and you have found your strength in Me. You have seen My goodness on the right hand and on the left. You have beheld My power, and My glory has not been hidden from you.

I have blessed you out of the bounties of heaven and have not withheld from you what your heart has desired. Yes, and I would do still more. For have I not promised that you *and* your household should be saved? Wasn't the blood applied to the lintel and the doorposts for the salvation of the entire family? (see Exodus 12:22–23)

So renew your energies, and know that I am working with you. For surely a light will shine out of the darkness, and the faith you have exercised through the years will be rewarded one hundredfold. So your faith will be turned to sight, for you will see with your eyes and hear with your ears and rejoice in your heart over what will come to pass.

I will do a wonderful work, and you shall praise and glorify My name *together!* For He that keeps you neither slumbers nor sleeps. The Lord your God is your strength, and in Him is no weariness. He never tires of you coming to Him, and your cry is welcome to His ears however frequent.

Cast yourself upon His mercies; for His loving-kindness never fails, and His grace and compassion are inexhaustible. His faithfulness is extended to all generations (see Isaiah 59:21).

LORD GOD, YOU ARE MY GOD;
MY HOPE IS IN YOU.
YOU WILL NEVER LEAVE ME NOR FORSAKE ME.
YOU WILL BRING ME THROUGH,
AND I WILL PRAISE YOUR NAME!

I Shall Gather My People

For the time has come for judgment to begin at the house of God;
and if it begins with us first, what will be the end of those
who do not obey the gospel of God?

1 PETER 4:17

Arise. Get up to the rim of the chasm, and look, and write what you see. For death and destruction, darkness and thick mists, and the cries of those who perish will rise, but there is none to hear. There is none to answer.

As it is written: Today is the day of salvation (2 Corinthians 6:2), and again: "Seek the LORD while He may be found" (Isaiah 55:6), for the night comes. Then My wrath will be poured out upon the ungodly, and there will be no hand stretched forth to save.

I have called to you in mercy, and in patience I have stretched out My hands to a careless and rebellious people. I have spoken from heaven, and My words have been ignored. I have cried out to them through My prophets, and their hearts have been as molten stone.

They have lifted up their voices in defiance against Me, but there will be none to deliver. There is no salvation in their hands, but they will go down together. They shall perish together in their folly. Behold, the day of mercy is at an end, and the Day of Judgment has come.

Lift your eyes to the clouds, for the heavens are filled with glory. Yes, He comes with ten thousand of His saints. Lift your hearts, for you will not be afraid of those things that are coming to pass upon the earth. FOR I SHALL GATHER MY PEOPLE TO MYSELF; and in the hour of destruction, I will stretch forth My hand to deliver them. In the hour of wrath, I will snatch away My own—My Beloved—and the flames will not touch them.

Surely My love is deep and abiding, constant and tender. I have not changed. For though nation rises against nation, and though war breaks out into a universal holocaust, although humanity in its folly dashes itself to bits against the wall of the inevitable, I still have not changed.

My heart is still tender. My thoughts toward you are still thoughts of loving-kindness. I look upon you with a deeper love than ever before. As the bridegroom anticipating the approaching wedding makes last-minute preparations and longs for the hour of fulfillment, so does My heart yearn for you, My Bride, My Beloved.

Though you see terror on every hand, only with your eyes will you look and see the reward of wickedness. I shall preserve you and keep you, and you shall walk with Me in white.

CHECK YOUR COURSE

And a great windstorm arose,
and the waves beat into the boat. . . .
They awoke Him and said to Him, "Teacher,
do You not care that we are perishing?"
Then He arose and rebuked the wind, and said to the sea,
"Peace, be still!" And the wind ceased
and there was a great calm.

MARK 4:37–39

There is never a day, there is never an hour, there is never a moment when you are outside My thoughts. As David said, "The Lord thinks upon me" (Psalm 40:17). You can say this as surely as David could. You are no less dear to My heart, and I am equally concerned for you.

Do not take the path of folly, for My heart goes with you wherever you go; and I grieve over you when you are turned aside. You may not be going in the opposite direction. You may even be on a road that lies quite parallel with the one I would have you travel. But to be almost in the perfect will of God is to miss it completely.

As the Scripture says: "Other little boats were also with Him"—but Jesus was in only one. Check your course. Chart it by My Word, and hold to it with rigid determination and do not be led aside by the other "little boats."

Be sure you are in the boat with Him if you hope to make it safe to shore in spite of the storms. For there will be storms; but you will be safe if you abide close with Me.

✛

Set Your Heart to Follow to the End

For he who sows to his flesh will of the flesh reap corruption,
but he who sows to the Spirit will of the Spirit reap everlasting life.

GALATIANS 6:8

Show Me your hand. I have fashioned it to bring glory to My Name. For My Name is above every Name, and praise and glory belong to Me, and in Me every living thing shall rejoice. For I will cause a light to shine out of the darkness, and in that place where you have walked in defeat, there I will cause victory to break forth.

Rise, arise, and put on your strength, for you are a people called by My Name, and in My Name you will be strong and accomplish great things. And I will bless you out of the abundance of heaven.

My strength shall be your delivering power. For I, the Lord, am in your midst, to be a mighty power to you, and there shall be no one weak among you. But the one who has more abundant grace will lend a lifting hand to the one who has less; and the one whose heart rejoices will cheer those who languish.

I know your works. Your heart has been an open book My Spirit has read. Yes, and I know your every desire, and I know your every need, and I go before you, and I shall bring it to pass.

In the morning, lift your heart in song. In the evening, let your requests be made known. And My peace will keep you, and My grace shall be your support.

Turn away from the diverging path; never fear to follow Me. For as the shepherd leads his sheep, you will know with certainty that I go before you. I will bring you to a place of broad pastures, of enlarged vision, of increased fruitfulness, and abounding blessings—and nothing shall prevent Me.

Do not look to your own thoughts, but walk in the Spirit; so will you accomplish the work the Spirit desires to do. Eternity alone will reveal the fruit of this hidden ministry. For we do not labor in the material realm, and we do not work with the elements of this world; but our labor is in the realm of the Spirit, and the accomplishments are not judged by natural sight, but will be revealed in the light of eternity.

Therefore be diligent. Follow Me so closely that there will be no distance between us. Listen carefully to My voice so you do not go your own way. For My path shines more and more brightly until that day. Set your heart to follow to the end, for at the end there awaits an exceeding weight of glory for those who endure.

✣

BREAK LOOSE THE FETTERS

But you shall receive power when the Holy Spirit has come upon you; and you shall be witnesses to Me. . .to the end of the earth.

ACTS 1:8

Behold, with a strong and mighty hand I will bring My people out. Yes, as I brought the children of Israel out from the bondage of Egypt and Pharaoh; with a yet greater form of liberation I will bring My people out from under the yoke of false prophets and the shackles of legalism. *For My people shall be a free people.* My people will obey Me, not a human leader. My people shall not labor in vain in the straw and stubble of the works of the flesh. My people shall walk in newness of life, and they shall be energized and led by My Spirit.

Through the Red Seas, through the Wildernesses, through the Jordans, through the Promised Lands of spiritual conquest—I am with My people. *Let no fear dismay.* Let no aspect of the past be a hindrance or stumbling block. I bring you out of

(85)

dead works into Living Reality. I bring you out of traditions of the past into fresh revelations of Myself in this Present Hour.

The past I use for your instruction, but not as a blueprint of the present nor as guidance for the future. Do not be afraid to follow Me. Indeed, if you knew how close I am standing to the "curtain of time," you would draw very near and be filled with expectancy. For one of these days—so very soon—the curtain will be drawn; the heavens will be rolled back; the canopy of the sky as you know it will be lifted away; and the Son of Man shall be revealed in power and great glory.

Then will My Church be as a diadem upon My head, tangible evidence of My kingship and victory. What sort of people ought you to be with such a prospect in view!

BREAK LOOSE THE FETTERS. Cast off the fears. Walk forth in Me in the conquering strength of My Holy Spirit.

A Garden of Fountains

The LORD will guide you continually, And satisfy your soul in drought,
And strengthen your bones; You shall be like a watered garden,
And like a spring of water, whose waters do not fail.

ISAIAH 58:11

Behold, My hand is upon you to bless you and to accomplish all My good purpose. For *this hour* I have prepared your heart, and in My kindness I will not let you fail.

Only relinquish *all* things into My hands; for I can work freely only as you release Me by complete committal—both of yourself and others. As was written of old: "Commit your way to the LORD, trust also in Him, and He shall bring it to pass" (Psalm 37:5). I will be your sustaining strength; and My peace shall garrison your mind. Only TRUST ME—all I do is done in love.

Adversities are a necessity. They are part of the pattern of life's pilgrimage for every individual; and who can escape them? But I say to you, that for those who walk in Me, and for those who are encircled by the intercessory prayers of My children, I will make of the suffering, yes, I will make of the trials a steppingstone to future blessing (see 2 Corinthians 4:17, 18).

My arms are around you, and never have I loved you more! I will make you like a garden of fountains whose streams are fed by the mountain springs.

An Instrument of Praise

In returning and rest you shall be saved;
In quietness and confidence shall be your strength.

ISAIAH 30:15

O. My child, I have chosen you for Myself, that I may make you an instrument of praise in My hand. I will bring forth from you a melody of praise and rejoicing, and cause the harp strings of your soul to vibrate with a joyful song.

Bless Me with your lips, and whisper My Name in adoration. I will free you from the prison house, and you will exalt your God in liberty of spirit.

How can you say to Me, "I am insignificant and unworthy"? No, you are precious to Me, you are the apple of My eye.

Do not turn back in unbelief, but press onward and upward until the darkness is left behind and you come out into the light. You will see Me then face-to-face, and know Me as your dearest friend.

Bring Me all that puzzles you. Many questions need no answer, for when the heart is at one with the Father, there comes an illumination of Spirit that transcends thought. Understanding becomes a state of heart rather than an achievement of the mind.

Learn to worship and you will have rest of soul; you will rise to a new place of fellowship, where you will be as the writer of the letter to the Ephesians said: made to "sit together in the heavenly places in Christ Jesus" (Ephesians 2:6).

You will be taught by the Spirit. Yes, He will open the mysteries of the Word to you. For it was by the Spirit of God that the Scriptures were given to holy men of old; even so, by the Spirit will the treasures of the Word be revealed to you.

LAUNCH OUT!

Casting down arguments and every high thing
that exalts itself against the knowledge of God,
bringing every thought into captivity to the obedience of Christ.

2 CORINTHIANS 10:5

LAUNCH OUT!

My people, you have touched only the fringes.

Yes, you have lingered on the shorelines.

Launch out on the vast sea of

My love and mercy, yes,

My mighty power and limitless resources.

For if you would enter into all that I have for you,

you must walk by faith upon the waters.

You must forever relinquish your doubts;

and your thoughts of self-preservation

you must forever cast aside.

For I will carry you, and I will sustain you by My power

in the ways that I have chosen and prepared for you.

You shall not take even the first step in your own strength.

For you are not able in yourself—

even as flesh is always unable to walk the way of the Spirit.

But My arm shall uphold you,

and the power of My Spirit shall bear you up.

Yes, you will walk upon the waves,
and the storm will only drive you more quickly
to the desired port.

Chart and compass you shall not need,
for My Spirit will direct your goings,
and are not the winds held in My fists?

Be not fearful but believing.

I Shall Put New Songs in your Mouth

O my soul, wait upon God, and He will do you good.

    Yes, He will refresh your soul.

For His tender mercies are never failing,

    and His kindness toward you is as the morning.

As the Sun of Righteousness shall arise

        with healing in His wings (see Malachi 4:2),

    so shall your God be unto you.

For the night is past; yes, I bring you into a new place:

a place of rejoicing in Me such as you have not known as yet.

For I shall fill your soul with fatness,

    and I will be with you to do you good.

    I will make your hands ready for war,

    and I will make your lips praise Me with songs.

I will put new songs in your mouth,

and you shall rejoice in the LORD your God

        for He is a mighty God.

    He delivers, and no man can bind.

    He lifts up, and none can pull down.

Yes, He acts valiantly, and who can prevent Him?

From Center
to Circumference

Lo, you seek revival.

You do well; only do not seek it in the energy of the flesh.

For the flesh is intent upon its own interests;

yes, it lusts after those things

that perish with the using.

I would have you seek Me in Spirit;

then I will come down upon you in all My fullness, and

will hold back nothing of all that I desire to do for you.

For My ways are hidden from those who

seek Me in the energy of the flesh.

Deep calls unto deep at the noise of the waterspouts (see Psalm 42:7), and I *am in you,* yes, *for this very purpose* above all other purposes, have I taken up My abode WITHIN you; that My Spirit might be diffused through your spirit, and that we might be one even as I am one with the Father.

I in you, and you in Me,

that we might be unified in thought and in action:

in devotion and in purpose,

that we might move continually not as two, but as ONE.

I ask you not to DO, but to BE.

For whatsoever is of the flesh is flesh;

but when you allow My Spirit to have *free course,* when you cease
to interfere with My moving within you,

then those things that shall be accomplished

both *within* and *through* you

will be truly the LIFE OF GOD.

For My Spirit is the Spirit of Life,

and My Spirit is the motivating power of Divine energy.

ALL ELSE IS DEATH. As it is written,

"Flesh and blood CANNOT inherit the Kingdom of God"

(see 1 Corinthians 15:50).

Neither can man through any endeavor of his own,

however holy his purpose,

produce this life, which does not exist

apart from the direct activity of the Spirit of God.

For I am WITH you and I am IN you
to make you neither barren nor unfruitful.

I am in YOU to give you Life,

and to give it to you ABUNDANTLY,

yes, LIFE WITHOUT LIMIT.

For all I am able to do for you is limited only by My

    omnipotence and My eternal, everlasting

        Life and Power,

    and to these THERE ARE NO LIMITS!

        Lo, I wait to bless you;

        I wait to give you of My fullness.

        I delight to do for you,

    because I love you beyond your power to begin to know.

Only drop those things you grasp in your hand,

        and place your hands in Mine.

Only pull your eyes from those things you hold precious,

        and I will fill them with My glory.

        Release your affections from all others.

          Place in My hands those you hold dear.

          Leave them in My keeping:

    for so shall your heart be set free to seek Me

        without distraction.

For when I am to you more precious than all else;

    when I have become more real to you than all else;

and when you love Me more than you love any other,

    then shall you know *complete satisfaction.*

Your peace shall flow as a river,
and your joy shall overflow as a fountain,
and My glory shall be poured out as the fragrant anointing oil
upon all your other relationships.

For I do NOT intend to strip you of earthly ties and joys,
but I long to have you give Me the center of your life
that My blessing may flow out to the circumference.
For My Spirit moves not from the circumference to the center,
but from the *center* to the *circumference*.

So yield to Me your inmost consciousness.
Offer Me not some random portion of your affections,
but give Me that deepest portion of your heart,
yes, that which seems to be your very life itself.
In truth it is so.
For you yield Me your life only as you offer Me your love.
For this reason I have said love is the fulfillment of the law.
So give Me WHOLLY your heart's affections,
and I will meet your every need.

Seek FIRST the Kingdom of Heaven;

set your desires wholly to obtain the riches of God,

and all other things shall be freely supplied

as the needs arise.

Only be very diligent in the quest,

for the enemy always lays in wait

that he may through evil device turn you aside.

Be not overtaken by his wiles.

Set your face like flint.

Lay aside every weight and deliberately remove

every hindrance.

Give yourself to prayer.

You have My word, yes, you have My promise,

that those who seek shall FIND.

And My promises are sure,

and My Word shall never pass away.

RAIN

O My child, I love you, I love you.

Go to the hills and look, for lo, the rain is coming.

The drought is over and past, and the sound

  of rain approaches!

    Yes, I will send showers of blessing

    upon the hearts of my waiting people;

  for before they call, I have prepared an answer,

  and while they are seeking Me,

    I shall come down upon them.

    O Lord, tarry not. We wait for You.

    We long for You. Yes, our souls pant for You

    as the thirsting deer pants for the water brooks

      (see Psalm 42:1).

    For we desire You with an unrelinquishing desire;

    yes, we cannot be denied, for there is no alternative.

O My child, I love you, I love you.

Lift your eyes to the heavens, for lo, they are filled with clouds;

yes, they are heavy with water.

  Get back to the camp.

  Set out the buckets and make preparation:

for already the wind rises, the leaves rustle in the trees;
the birds hasten to their nests, and lo, I come.

> I come to revive and to refresh.

> I come to quicken and to cleanse.

> I come as floods upon parched ground.

So shall new life spring forth,
and the desert shall be filled with flowers.

> For since time was, I have never forsaken My people.

> I have undertaken for them; I have protected them.

> I have delivered them in every time of need.

> I have rescued them from every calamity.

I have denied them nothing of the desires of their hearts.

> They have not always asked in wisdom,

> but I have never failed to respond (see Psalm 106:15).

Do you think I love My Church less than I loved
> ancient Israel?

Do you think I stretched forth My hand for them,
and through mighty miracles set them free from the bondage
of Pharaoh, and made them a way to escape through the Red
Sea, and provided for their daily needs through the wilderness
journey, and gave them water out of the Rock,
> and will do any less for *you*?

For you are twice beloved.

You are My body, the Church, and you are My Chosen Bride.

Yes, your slightest wish is My command.

For I delight to please you,

even as a bridegroom seeks to please his bride.

How much MORE do I long to bestow upon you tokens of My affection? And My love for you surpasses all human comprehension.

For I am not a man that I should be limited;

and I need not divide My Spirit among many,

but I long to share with EACH My fullness;

and there is no favoritism in My love.

Look not upon your lack of capacity, for I will

enlarge your heart.

Open not your mouth to question Me,

for love questions not, but receives gladly and freely.

As you do the same, you will not be disappointed.

Be not dismayed,

neither give heed to your sense of unworthiness,

for lo, I have loved you *simply because I have loved you*,

and what other reason do I need?

Do you not yourself do the same in human relations?
Shall I not shed My love upon you for no other reason
than simply that I have chosen to do so?
Otherwise it was not love in its purest sense.

For only as you know with certainty
that I love you *though you bring no gift,*
can you return to Me love that will remain constant,
both when I bless, and when I withhold.

Lo, You are mine. You have dove's eyes.
Kiss me with the kisses of Your lips,
for Your lips are sweeter than honey.
Gather me in Your embrace,
for Your arms are stronger than the bands of Orion
(see Job 38:31).
All eternity is held in one moment in Your presence,
and all of time is empty apart from Your fellowship.

SHALL I COMMEND YOU?

Behold, is it a small thing that you should weary the Lord God Almighty with your complaints?

Is it a light thing in My eyes that you walk in weakness when I have made full provision that you might appropriate My strength?

Have you not insulted Me in that I have condescended to dwell within you, and you have set Me aside, and quenched and grieved My Holy Spirit and walked in your own ways?

Shall I commend you?
Shall you escape My rebuke and displeasure?
You look in vain for My smile.
For you think in your heart
      that you can bring Me some gift.

"I will do Him a kindness," you have said, and you thought I would accept this as devotion.

Do not deceive yourself. God is not to be toyed with.
"See," you have crooned, "I have brought you this basket
      of fruit."
            Cursed be the ground that brought it forth!
Have I not required blood? But you have loathed sacrifice.

And I have said I will have none of your pretty gifts, for God desires integrity, and to obey is better than all your vain attempts to appease.

Behold, I am angry with you, and not without cause.
You have profaned My sanctuary with vain endeavors in the flesh.
You do not come to Me in spirit and in truth; but you have set limits of your own making to check and hinder Me.
You say you fear to offend;
but I say to you, for the very hardness and willfulness of your own hearts, you will not yield Me control.
You keep it in your own hands lest
your iniquities are uncovered and your shame appears to all.

Lo, I will have none of it.
I will come to you when you have humbled yourself.
I will purge your sins when you put away your sham and hypocrisy.
I will gather you to My heart when you shall cease loving your own self.

The days are short.
Do you want me to come to you with a rod or in love?

My Energizing Power

O My child, I have waited long for your coming.

My eyes have grown weary with watching,

and My heart heavy with longing for you.

For I have said, "Rest in Me," but you have striven.

I have said, "Stand still," but you have continued to run.

I have called, but you have been listening to human voices.

Turn to Me.

You do not need to do more. For you will find

your quest ended.

Then you will see how futile has been all the struggle.

Like the sinner who misses the gift of saving grace

through absorption in good works,

so you, My child, have missed My sweet reality

in your frantic effort to please Me.

As Martha in her desire to minister to Me forfeited

My nearness,

so you have done.

My child, I have need of nothing. I desire only your love.

Give Me this first always, and whatsoever service may follow,

you will then do with light feet and a heart set free.

Abandon to Me your whole being,

and I will then work in and through you in such a way

that even as I am using you,

you shall simultaneously experience My energizing power;

so that in the very process of giving,

you will in very truth receive even beyond what you give,

and will in each instance emerge richer and stronger.

There is no loss when you serve Me thus.

For when your life is wholly lost in My life, there is never

anything but gain.

As the prophet of old exclaimed,

"They go from strength to strength" (see Psalm 84:7).

Only sin works death and loss. Righteousness works life and

health.

So come first to Me.

Yes, come until the stream of your life

is swallowed up in the ocean of My fullness.

Then you will go, and you will give,

and in your giving you will never know lack.

The Lord is your shepherd; you shall not want

(see Psalm 23:1).

For the kingdom of God is righteousness and peace

and joy in the Holy Spirit (see Romans 14:17).

A Song at Midnight

Behold, I am near at hand to bless you,
and I will surely give to you out of the abundance of heaven.

For My heart is open to your cry; yes,
when you cry to Me in the night seasons,

I am alert to your call, and when you search after Me,
the darkness will not hide My face;
it will be as the stars which shine more brightly in the
deep of night.

Even so it shall be. In the night of spiritual battle,
there I shall give you fresh revelations of Myself,
and you shall see Me more clearly than you could
in the sunlight of ease and pleasure.
Man by nature chooses the day and shuns the night;
but I say to you,
I shall make your midnight a time of great rejoicing,
and I will fill the dark hour with songs of praise.
Yes, with David, you shall rise at midnight to sing.

It has been written, "Joy comes in the morning,"
but I will make your song break out in the night.
For he who lifts the shout of faith and praise *in the night*,
to him there *shall* be joy in the morning.

KEEP YOUR FACE TOWARD THE SUNRISE

Behold, I have sent you out alone,

but I have gone ahead to prepare your way;

yes, through the darkness to bear a light.

I ask you only to follow Me,

for I will surely lead you in a safe path,

though dangers lurk on every hand.

Yes, I will be your protection.

I will be your comfort.

I will be your joy.

I will turn the bitter tear to sweet perfume.

By My Spirit, I will mend the broken heart.

I will pour warm, fragrant oil into the deep wound.

For My heart is fused with your heart,

and in your grief, I am one with you.

Yes, I will fill the vacant place.

My arms shall hold you, and you will not fall.

My grace shall sustain you, and you will not faint.

My joy shall fortify your spirit

even as a broken body is rejuvenated by a blood transfusion.

My smile shall dispel the shadows,

and My voice shall speak courage.

Yes, I will surely keep you, and you will not know fear.

You shall rest your foot upon the threshold of heaven.

I shall hide you in My pavilion.

You shall have My constant care.

I will not leave you for a moment.

I will keep you from despair:

I will deliver you from confusion.

When you are perplexed,

I will guide you in wisdom and in judgment.

By your light others shall be led out of the valley.

By your courage the weak shall be lifted up.

By your steadfastness he that wavers shall be stabilized.

Lo, the hour is upon you.

Do not look back.

Keep your face toward the sunrise,

For He shall rise fresh daily in your soul

with healing in His wings.

———

Under every burden, God will slip His hand—

Every gulf of sorrow, His great love has spanned.

Into every heartache, God will pour His balm;

Ease the pain and anguish, bring a blessed calm.

Your Body,
A Living Sacrifice

Yield Me your body as a living sacrifice,

and do not be conformed to the things of the world,

but be transformed by the renewal of your mind

(see Romans 12:1–2a).

Set your affections on things of the Spirit,

and do not be in bondage to the desires of the flesh.

For I have purchased you at great price.

Yes, you are My special possession and My treasure.

I would have you set your affections and desires upon Me

even as I have set My heart upon you.

It is written that the wife has no power over her own body

except for the husband, nor the husband but for the wife

(see 1 Corinthians 7:4).

So I would that you should yield your body to Me,

otherwise I am limited in My power to work.

For I must have a vessel through which to operate.

I would have you be a vessel not only yielded to me, but puri-

fied, dedicated, sanctified for My use; available to Me at all

times, and ready to be used at whatever time I have

need of you.

You will not have time to make yourself ready when I need you.

You must be prepared.

You must keep yourself in a state of readiness.

You cannot live to the flesh and at the same time be available
to the Spirit.

You must walk in the Spirit, and in so doing
keep yourself from becoming entangled in worldly things.

You must live in obedience to the Spirit,
and thus be kept from being in bondage to your carnal nature.

I Myself cannot keep you except you first make
this choice.

It was concerning this matter that Jude wrote his word of admonition: "But you, beloved, building yourselves up on your most holy faith, praying in the Holy Spirit, keep yourselves in the love of God" (Jude 20–21).

As you set your soul through *deliberate choice of your will* to pursue the worship of God by praying in the Spirit,

you will find your faith strengthened
and your life bathed in the love of God.

With your faith laying hold on God's promises and power,
and your actions motivated by the love of God,
you will find yourself in the path of the *activity of God;*

His blessing shall be upon you,
and He will accomplish His works through you.

You do not need to make plans nor resort to any
 clever strategy.
 Keep yourself in the love of God.
Pray in the Spirit. Rejoice evermore. Set your affections
 upon Christ.
 God will do through you and for His glory such things
as it pleases Him to do, and you will rejoice with Him.
For as your own spirit is aware when His Spirit is grieved
 within you, so will you also be aware when His Spirit
 rejoices within you. This is His joy. This is the joy He
 promised.
 This is the greatest joy that can come to the human
heart, for it is the joy of God, and the joy of God transcends all
human joy.
 Surely you will not only rejoice but be exceeding glad,
 with a gladness surpassing your power to tell.
In this way you will give this back to Him,
 since no other can fully receive it,
 even as David poured out to Him
 the precious water from the well of Bethlehem
 (see 2 Samuel 23:15–16).

 Praise His wonderful Name!

Conviction and Forgiveness

Confess your trespasses to one another,
and pray for one another, that you may be healed.
The effective, fervent prayer of a righteous man avails much.

JAMES 5:16

My patience is running out. I have purposed and man has despised. I have planned and man has set at naught. I have willed and you have resisted me. Do not be smug in your own ways; for your ways are not My ways.

You are indulgent when I have called you to rigid discipline. You speak soft words when I would require you to speak the truth. You interfere with the convicting work of My Holy Spirit when you smooth over confession. I am not a severe God, unmindful of the frailties of human nature; but I am a God of divine love and holiness, and I desire your fellowship, and I long for you to know My joy.

Man cannot forgive sin. Why do you then excuse either yourself or your brother? Before Me you stand or fall. Confess your faults one to another, and pray for one another that you may be perfected. Rebuke, warn, and exhort each other with all longsuffering and patience. Love and forgive each other, but do not lighten conviction.

My love and holiness are beyond your comprehension. I do

not love you because you are sinless (how then could I love any?), but I am able to receive you into My fellowship and bring you close to My heart on the merits of the shed blood of the Lord Jesus Christ. Here rests your hope of cleansing and acceptance. Here is the only door of access between sinful man and a holy God. But here indeed is all you need.

Then why set about to excuse and rationalize your sins when the way of confession and forgiveness stands open to you? Do not hinder Me, for time is precious, and I am waiting for you.

Do Not Look Back

Behold, I have made you a nest in the hollow of My hand,
    and you shall lie down and sleep.
        Though the elements rage,
          though the winds blow and the floods come,
            you shall rest in peace.
For you are precious in My sight, O My child.
I know you by name, for you are not the child of a stranger,
        but the fruit of My own loins. Yes, I have begotten you,
I have called you by your name, and you are Mine.

Be not dismayed, for as I suffered,
        so shall you suffer in the world.
        I have not taken you out of the world,
but I am with you to help you and to encourage you, and to
give you strength in all you may be called upon to endure.

        You face each new day with Me at your side.
          (Never forget that I am there.)
        You meet every difficult circumstance
          with My arm outstretched to fight for you.

Do not lift your hand to attempt to accomplish any slightest
task in your own strength. This I have forbidden.
God helps not those who help themselves,
but He is the champion of those who cannot help
themselves,
and of those who are wise enough not to try.
It is not your cooperation for which I have asked,
but your submission.
Not that you go alone until you fall,
but that you draw upon My strength for *every step* —
both the smooth and the rough.

If you form the habit of trusting Me in the easy way,
you will find it the natural thing to lean upon Me
in the difficult situation.
And if I bring you through the river in summer,
you shall not fear to trust Me in flood time.

So clasp your hand in Mine, and do not loosen your hold.
For you cannot tell what great thing I may do for you
through some small happening.
Your every hair is numbered,
And the most incidental occurrences of the most ordinary day
I delight to choose and use to reveal
My earnestness in helping you.

Clasp Me to your heart,
for I love you with an everlasting love,
and with strong cords I have bound you.

Look not back, but look ahead,
for I have glory prepared for you.
Yes, when you look on My face
you will surely say that these present sufferings
are in no way comparable
to the glory I have in store for you.

FLING ASIDE YOUR FEARS

Lo, I have sought you,
following you upon the hills and pursuing you through the
barren wastes.
Yes, I have called after you, but you have not heard.
You thought in your heart that you would find Me,
and you have set out in your haste to seek for Me,
but you have looked for Me in vain.

You have scanned the horizon from day to day,
until your eyes fail you from your searching,
as a traveler seeking in vain for a spring in the desert,
and finding none languishes for water and faints in the heat.

Lo, like Hagar of old, your tears have blinded your eyes,
and meanwhile I have revealed My glory and made My provisions apparent to the child (see Genesis 21:17).
"Except you become as a little child,
you will in no way enter in" (see Luke 18:17).

My ways are hidden from those who seek Me in impatience,
and the eyes that seek Me in human wisdom will never
find Me.

For I am found by those who seek Me

in utter simplicity and in candid honesty.

Do not rebuke Me,

neither complain that I have left you alone.

Lo, I am at your side, but your fretfulness

has raised an iron curtain between us.

For when you are utterly finished

and exhausted in your struggling;

when you have come to the end of all your striving;

when you are ready to abandon your intellectual pursuit,

and when you cast yourself upon Me

as a baby upon its mother's breast;

then shall you know surely that I have been constantly

at your very side; that I have never deserted you.

Yes, My love for you is of such nature and intensity that
it would be impossible for you to ever escape My thoughts,
or for My longing for you to ever waver.

Cast aside your questionings.

Fling aside your fears.

For surely My arms are already outstretched to receive you.

Only believe.

For in the moment you relinquish *all*—

in that same moment you shall know release.

For you shall be set free of yourself

and shall be captive of My love.

My arms shall gather you, and I shall never let you go!

Run with Patience

O My child, there is nothing that I would hold back from you.

If you will heed My Word, if you will listen to My voice,

    I will surely lead you in a plain path.

Set your affections upon Me and keep them there.

    Center your attention upon Me.

Yes, set your heart to follow after Me with singleness of mind.

    This will remove all doubt at every crossroad.

    This will keep you continually at My disposal.

      Never set out upon a "project."

      My life is not project but overflow.

You have already witnessed the verdure of life that has sprung

forth where the waters of My Spirit have flowed.

    How can any doubt remain?

    But the flesh dies hard; it is true.

Even Jesus learned obedience through suffering and

    self-discipline (see Hebrews 5:8).

And Paul admonished: "Endure hardship as a good soldier"

      (2 Timothy 2:3).

    All that comforts the flesh weakens the Spirit.

I could by adversity strip from you the comforts of life,

    but I will bless you in double portion,

if of your own accord you do as the apostle Paul and lay aside

    every weight,

resisting the many temptations that continually beset you

    as you run with patience the course I set before you

    (see Hebrews 12:1).

    "Running" with "patience"—

in these two words I have combined the intensity of purpose

and the quiet waiting upon Me you must have, or else you will

be overtaken in the race by fatigue of body and soul.

    So as I have told you before,

Come to Me and pour out your praise and your love and your

worship. I will bless you and guide you and use you

    in My own good time and pleasure.

    You shall not be disappointed.

BE MUCH WITH ME

Therefore you also be ready,
for the Son of Man
is coming at an hour
you do not expect.

LUKE 12:40

My people, set the watch in the nighttime; yes, rise and pray, and do not let that hour come upon you unaware.

For the time is short; yes, the storm is gathering fast. You see clouds in the sky, and you say rain is approaching.

Can you not discern the events that are currently shaping up in the affairs of men, and be as keen to observe their portent and know that disaster and holocaust are in the making?

But you are prone to fall into the same snare as others—to presume that prosperity and peace will continue, simply because you wish so strongly that it might be so. You are not ignorant concerning the prophecies of My Word as some are, and yet you allow the feelings and attitudes that are abroad in the land to invade your own personal life.

Be more with Me, and let My Spirit pervade your spirit, and then you shall be more influenced by Me than by the world around you. But be prepared for the fact that you will then be of a different mind and attitude than those around you, and be willing to accept the difference and be able to ignore misunderstanding.

For many will not accept a message of warning, because they have set their own personal ambitions against the will of God, and they are so intent upon their own pursuits that they refuse to tolerate the thought of possible interference of any kind.

But you, beloved, be much with Me, for there is a great and heavy burden on My heart. For God takes no pleasure in the death of the wicked. My longsuffering and grace have continued because I deeply desire that all should come to repentance. But the grapes of wickedness are full, and the vats of the winepresses are already beginning to receive the juice, and before long they will be running full.

For the times of the Gentiles are drawing to a close, and I come. Be ready, for I come quickly.

$\mathcal{B}$E NOT AFRAID

O My child, rest in Me.

Yes, quietly settle down in My care, as a bird settles in a nest.

For I am watching over you, and in love I will care for you.

There is no danger with which I am unable to cope.

There is no enemy too formidable for Me to handle.

I am able to carry out all My purposes,

and to keep you at the same time.

Be not afraid;

neither allow terror to strike at your heart.

My power is at your disposal.

My presence stands around you,

and nothing can harm you so long as you are in My care,

and that is forever. . . .

Seize Each Opportunity

Behold, as the lilies of the field, and as the grass,
    so your life is but for a season.
Yes, though you flourish in health, yet your time is short.
    You have no sure promise of tomorrow.
Therefore live each day as though it were your last.
    Seize each opportunity, knowing that it may be the last.

For it is certainly true that no situation presents itself twice the
    same. The opportunities of today are not those of
    tomorrow.
Do not live as though they might be repeated.
    Do not fail to enter every open door, or be held back by
a feeling of unreadiness. I Myself am your preparation.

I will give you the needed grace and wisdom for each
    moment as it comes, and you will rejoice in the victory.
For I will overcome timidity, and I Myself will displace
    inadequacy.
    This is *My* work. I will do it Myself through you if you
allow yourself to be a channel for the flow of My Spirit.

For I Myself am the life. I Myself am your wisdom and your
strength,
even as I am your joy and your peace.
I am your victory. My word is power, because My word is
spirit and truth.

Do not bear needless burdens.
They will only press upon your spirit and interfere with My
movings.
Much remains to be accomplished.
Linger not over what appears to be an unfinished case. Pass on.
My Spirit will continue to strive though you give no further
thought. In this way your mind shall be kept free and your path
open,
and it shall always be a new way.
Keep moving always, and from life to life I will accomplish My
purpose.
And know that as I work, all things work together,
so that there is gathering strength, and there shall be a glorious
consummation. Praise God!

THE ART OF COMMITTAL

He heals the brokenhearted and binds up their wounds.

PSALM 147:3

O My child, lay your heart in My hand, and let Me heal it. Yes, let Me gather up your tears, for they are precious to Me (see Psalm 56:8). You have not been suffering alone, but I Myself have been near you all along the way. My heart has felt all that you have felt. You do not have a high priest who is not able to sympathize with your sufferings, but one who experienced every grief and human emotion common to all people. In the midst of these painful experiences, He did not sin. Therefore, He is one who is able to help you (see Hebrews 2:18).

He is one, who having walked the same path Himself, is able to teach you how, in the midst of these human experiences of hurts, frustrations, loneliness, and heartache, you may rise above the natural tendencies to fall into the sins of self-pity, self-reproach, depression of spirit, resentment, and the like.

It is not easy. Not only is it not easy, but in the natural, in the flesh, it is impossible. But the same grace I promised to the apostle Paul to help him bear his affliction, this same grace I will give to you (see 2 Corinthians 12:9).

You may bring the whole of your burden to Me. I will help you as the days go by, and as the trials come and go; and as the learning process continues, I will teach you the spiritual secrets of the art of committal.

For in complete and repeated committal lies the key to victories that can be thus more easily won, less painfully achieved, and more quickly gained, so that the valleys become less deep and less dark, and more quickly passed through.

"Man is born," it is written, "to trouble, as the sparks fly upward" (Job 5:7). This is true as surely as rain falls and snow is cold. But it is equally true, and gloriously so, that I have promised to deliver you out of all your troubles.

So will you now take the first step in this experience of committal, and give Me your heart?

Make it as tangible a transaction as possible, and visualize your own hand laying the physical organ of your heart in My hands. Say to Me, "Take this, Loving Master and Wonderful Lord, and do with it as pleases You."

WHATSOEVER YOU SOW

He who sows sparingly will also reap sparingly, and he who sows
bountifully will also reap bountifully. . . He who supplies seed to the
sower, and bread for food, supply and multiply the seed you have sown
and increase the fruits of your righteousness.

2 CORINTHIANS 9:6–10

How can I give you healing for your body while there is anxiety in your mind? So long as there is disease in your thoughts, there will be disease in your body. You need many things, but one thing in particular you must develop for your own preservation, and that is an absolute confidence in My loving care.

It is written, "Come to Me, all you who labor and are heavy laden, and I will give you rest" (Matthew 11:28). Only when your mind is at rest can your body build health. Worry is an actively destructive force. Anxiety produces tension, and tension is the road to pain. Fear is devastating to the physical well-being of the body. Anger throws poison into the system that no antibiotic can ever counteract.

"Be sure your sin will find you out," the Bible states (Numbers 32:23). One of the most common ways that hidden sin is revealed is through the maladies of the body. Resentments and ill will bring about more arthritis than is caused by wrong diet. More asthma is caused by repressed fury than by pollen or cat fur.

There was no illness in the body of Jesus because there was no sin in His soul. There was weariness as a natural result of labor and sacrificial service, but there was no undue fatigue and exhaustion brought on by anxiety.

Ten minutes of unbridled temper can waste enough strength to do a half day of wholesome work. Your physical energy is a gift from God, entrusted to you to be employed for His glory. It is a sin to take His gift and dissipate it through the trap doors of the disposition's evil emotions.

Do not condemn others for jeopardizing their health by harmful habits and wasting their energies on vain pursuits while you undermine your health by unworthy emotions. You waste time by entertaining such things as self-pity and remorse and evil surmising when you might be keeping your mind in an attitude of praise and faith. Your mind could be constructively employed, but instead you allow this to be a period of destructive action.

You cannot risk giving your thoughts free rein. They will never choose the right path until you bridle them and control them by your own disciplined will. You are master of your own house. You do not have to invite into your mind the foul birds of evil thoughts and allow them to nest there and bring forth their young.

Whatsoever you sow in your secret thought life, that you will reap. Sow love and kindness, and you shall be rewarded openly. Sow charity and forgiveness, and you shall reap in kind. Sow generosity and gratitude, and you shall never feel poor. Sow hope, and you shall reap fulfillment. Sow praise, and you shall reap joy and well-being and a strong faith. Sow bountifully, and you shall reap bountifully. Sow! You shall see your seed and be satisfied.

CHASTENING

*You are the salt of the earth; but if the salt loses its flavor,
how shall it be seasoned? It is then good for nothing but
to be thrown out and trampled underfoot by men.*

MATTHEW 5:13

Have I not said that unless you experience chastening, you may well doubt your sonship? Why then should you shrink from My rod of correction? You are not the teacher, but the pupil; not the parent, but the child; not the vine, but the branch.

Discipline and correction must come if you desire to be brought into conformity to My divine will. Shun nothing My hand brings to bear upon your life. Accept My blessings and My comfort, but do not despise My stern dealings. All are working toward your ultimate perfection.

Do you hope to be made perfect apart from the corrective process? Do you expect to bear fruit abundantly without the pruning process? No, My children, either bend in submission to My hand, or you will break in rebellion.

Godly sorrow yields the good fruit of repentance, but if you are brittle and unyielding, you will know a grief of spirit for which there is no remedy. Keep a flexible spirit, so that I may mold you and shape you freely, teach you readily, and not be detained by your resistance.

I need disciplined Christians. To entertain self-will is to court disqualification. You cannot do My work to My satisfaction except you do it in accordance with My specifications. There are not many blueprints for one building; there is only one. Even so, I am the husbandman. If you refuse My loving care, you will be cut down by others who have no concern for your soul. As I said of the salt: If it loses its flavor, it is good for nothing but to be trodden underfoot (see Matthew 5:13). If the branch bears no fruit, people will gather it and burn it (see John 15:1–6).

Do not relax in a false peace. Do not negate My love by refusing My discipline. My love is not indulgence. I have much to accomplish in fulfilling My will. I cannot pamper your will when it is running counter to Mine.

Do not continue to be spoiled children, allowing the emotions of the old nature to invade your spiritual fellowships. While there are jealousies and competition and suspicions, you are yet allowing the carnal nature to reign—even to infiltrate your spiritual gifts.

THE LAST GREAT OUTPOURING

"I am the Alpha and the Omega, the Beginning and the End,"
says the Lord, "who is and who was and who is to come, the Almighty."

REVELATION 1:8

Behold, you stand on the threshold of a new day. For I have truly great things in store for you. Yes, you have not power to conceive what I am about to do. For I will bring to pass a new thing. You will rejoice exceedingly. You have heard of the showers, but I say to you: I will send a mighty downpour. Many have cried out to Me from hungry hearts and have received of My fullness and seen My glory; but I say to you: in the day of the great deluge which is coming, many will come to know the reality of My power who have until now not even dreamed of such a thing.

Many who are scoffers and many who are honest doubters will find themselves swept away on the swelling tide of the outpouring of the Holy Spirit. For this is the time of the last great outpouring. This is the day of preparation for the coming of the Lord. Many shall rejoice together in the Spirit's work who are now at sword's point over doctrinal disputes and barriers of tradition.

But let your heart be encouraged; for a new day is dawning:

a day of repentance and a day of gathering for My people. For they shall not continue to be barricaded and isolated behind walls of prejudice. I am the LORD, and I will be worshiped in spirit and in truth, and not in the bigotry of sectarianism and narrowness of denominationalism. The world is waiting for a robust Church to minister to its needs; and how can an ailing, dismembered Body bring healing to a sick and dying world?

Surely I will pour out My Spirit, and by prophecies, by signs and wonders, by many different types of miracles, and by healings, I will reaffirm the veracity of My Word and bring the message of the Gospel of Redemption to many who would otherwise never give heed. I am the Alpha and the Omega. Stand firm in Me. Never waver.

Be faithful regardless of apparent failures and discouragements; for My word shall surely be fulfilled, and your eyes shall see revival in proportions such as never before witnessed in the history of the human race.

Keep your eye on the end of the course. Victory is secured already. Do not let the hurdles cause you consternation. Stay in the running. Truly, I am at your side. According to each day shall your strength be; and the race is not won by the swift, but the obedient shall receive the prize.

Sing, My Children

I will praise the Lord according to His righteousness,
And will sing praise to the name of the Lord Most High.

PSALM 7:17

O My people, My chosen ones, I love you with an everlasting love, and with the cords of My faithfulness I have bound you to Myself. I am not a man that I should lie (see Numbers 23:19), but all I have promised, I will surely do, so that the Father may be glorified in you, and that you may bear much fruit.

I have promised you My grace, in order that you may extend to others love like Mine, which flows forth in the face of hostility. When you were an enemy of God, Christ died for you. Calvary love was given not only for friends but also for enemies. I want to teach you how to love with Calvary love.

Remember that I am in the midst of you when you praise Me. Never let any kind of anxiety crowd out your praise. Do not be concerned for My reputation. I have withstood many storms, and I will survive this one. Human strivings are like the waters around Gibraltar. They have beat upon the rock, but they have not changed it. I am not disturbed, and I forbid you to be anxious.

For anxiety produces tension, and tension erodes joy; and when joy is gone, victory is lost, faith is weakened, and spontaneity is destroyed. The spirit falls ill. The salt has lost its flavor. Its savor is a saver. What can I use to preserve My work in your midst if you lose your joy?

Rejoice *always*, said the apostle Paul—and again I say *rejoice*. Let your stability be apparent to all, for truly, the coming of the Lord is near. Prepare yourselves, and be strong; for it is the Lord who upholds you and He it is who gives you the victory.

Sing, My children, and let the shout of praise be heard: for the Lord is mighty, and His Name is glorious.

LEARN TO REIGN

*Till we all come to the unity of the faith
and of the knowledge of the Son of God, to a perfect man,
to the measure of the stature of the fullness of Christ.*

EPHESIANS 4:13

"Tender Dove"

Holy Spirit from above,
Tender, undefiled Dove,
In my spirit have Thy way,
O'er my actions hold full sway.

Blest Companion from on high,
In Thy comfort ever nigh;
Bind my heart to Christ in love,
O Thou precious, Heavenly Dove.

This cold heart and these dull eyes,
So unfit for Paradise,
Fire with Thy sacred flame,
Show the power of Jesus' Name.

Weak I in myself may be,
But my strength shall be in Thee.
Sweet provision of God's grace;
In Thy gift His love I trace.

I could not Thy coming earn,
Could no more Thy wooing spurn.
Take control and bless and use
As the Infinite shall choose.

QUIET POOL

Wait upon ME.
Let your life be as a deep, quiet pool.
Let your heart rest in My hand as a bird in a nest.
Let your eyes be still. Let your hands be free.
For then I shall fill all your vision,
and then I shall take your hands into Mine
and My power shall flow forth into you.

If you would only make yourself a place apart,
yes, removed from the pressure and turmoil,
and there I will meet you. Yes, I wait for your coming.
For I long to pour out My blessings upon you,
and I long to give you My fullness.
Only be still before Me.
Never let the toils and cares of the day
rob you of this sweet fellowship with Me.

For I know what you need, and I am concerned about your
duties and responsibilities.
You will find your cares vanish,
and your load is lightened by an unseen hand.
I would have you bring Me your love,
and even as you are bringing Me your love,

I shall in turn bring to you My power,
so that I work for you in a twofold measure.

I will give you the power to discharge your duties with greater efficiency. I am actively engaged in working for you in ways you cannot see, to make your path clear, and to bring about things you could never accomplish, and which would otherwise absorb your energies and wear out your patience.

So I say again. . .Rest in Me. Wait upon Me.
Come apart with Me. Seek My face. Seek My fellowship.

O Lord, what shame that You should need to beg us thus! Better that others might find us unavailable because of our occupation with You, rather than for us to be so slow to come, so dull to hear, so cold of heart, so indolent of soul.

O God, spare us Your wrath!
Do not let Your anger be kindled against us.
Let us ask only one thing more, and do not turn away.

Grant this one prayer more, O Lord, that You would give us all that is lacking in us; intensify our hunger and fire our devotion; take the indifference from our spirits; and have within us Your wonderful way and perfect will, O God, we pray. Amen.

CALL OF THE TURTLEDOVE

When Elizabeth heard the greeting of Mary. . .the babe leaped in her womb; and Elizabeth was filled with the Holy Spirit.

LUKE 1:41

O My children, there is the sound of the turtledove echoing throughout the land. It is the voice of the Bridegroom calling His Bride. It is the wooing of the Spirit bringing forth a people for His Name. It is the Lord of Glory, Jesus Christ Himself, drawing together those who are His. It is the call of love, and those who truly love Him will respond.

Like attracts like; and love has always been the test of true discipleship. Those whose hearts are fixed on things above will not be held by worldly entanglements (even though they may be within the organized church). Those who are listening to the voice of their Beloved will not be deafened by the cries of men. In a world filled with noises, each demanding attention, they will hear Him.

Yes, they shall even hear the tender cooing of the turtledove! Another stand beside them and hear only the voice of the preacher. Another may be giving attention to the opinions and arguments of men. In the words of the beloved hymn writer: "The love of Jesus, what it is, None but His loved ones know."

You need not fear that you will miss it. Be it ever so soft, you shall hear. Your heart shall hear, and your heart shall leap with joy. You will be like Elizabeth when she was greeted by Mary. The response was immediate—an inner, involuntary response to the nearness of the Christ, even while He was yet unborn and unseen by the world.

I tell you, there shall be a revelation of My nearness given to My dear ones before My second coming.

Anticipate Me. Watch for Me. Your heart will listen, and your heart shall hear. I am not far off. I am looking through the lattice (see Song of Solomon 2:9). You shall see Me—you shall know—you shall rejoice.

$\mathcal{L}$OVE NEVER FAILS

Love never fails.

1 CORINTHIANS 13:8

Behold, I am the Lord, your God; is anything too hard for Me? I am the light of the world, and the greatest darkness will never be able to quench that light. I will be to you a cloud to preserve you by day and a pillar of fire to protect you by night. Both in sunshine and in darkness, I shall be near you. You will delight in Me in your joys; and in your difficulty My love for you shall be as inescapably real as a blazing pillar of fire. Yes, all I was to Israel and more I shall be to you. For have I not promised to give you the desires of your heart, and the nations for your inheritance (see Psalm 2:8)?

Let *no fear* hinder you. Whoever wavers will not receive. But be single-minded and rebuke every alien thought in My Name, for it comes from the enemy. He knows full well that he has no defense against pure faith. Only if he succeeds in planting seeds of doubt can he hold back the blessing of heaven among God's people and nullify the witness to the lost. So hold fast your profession of faith, for there is a great recompense of reward. (Or we might say, the inheritance of faith is a most rewarding recompense.)

So praise Me continually, for *praise* works *faith*, and *God inhabits the praise of His people.* If I seem to be far from you, praise! If darkness seems to press about you, know this—you have neglected to PRAISE ME. Love ME; pour out your adoration and worship. Be sure of this: LOVE NEVER FAILS. Loving Me never fails to bring Me to your side. He sees Me most clearly who loves Me most dearly.

$\mathcal{H}$old Fast

Looking unto Jesus, the author and finisher of our faith,
who for the joy that was set before Him endured the cross,
despising the shame,
and has sat down at the right hand of the throne of God.

HEBREWS 12:2

Hold fast that which you have, and let no one take your crown.

Let no one hinder you in pursuit of the reward.

Let nothing stand in the way of your complete victory.

Let no weariness or discouraging thought cause you to loosen the rope of faith, but bind it tighter and anchor fast to My Word.

My Word can never fail,

yes, and I will fulfill all My good promises. Have I not said, "He who seeks finds" (Matthew 7:8)? And have I not promised to reward those who diligently seek Me (see Hebrews 11:6)?

Not the dilatory seeker, but the diligent seeker. Not the one whose seeking is in reality only wishing, but the one who has grown so intent in his quest, so wholly absorbed, that he is unaware in his toiling of the sweat upon his brow.

To the extent that he has ceased reckoning the cost, indeed has quit offering bribes, as though the fullness of God could be purchased, and has set out on foot, deserting all else to follow the call of the Spirit until. . .

Until hunger is swallowed up in fullness. Until heart-cry is answered by the voice of God through His mighty Holy Spirit.

Until all the emptiness and loneliness of the subterranean recesses of his soul are flooded by the sublime, glorious reality of Emmanuel.

Emmanuel! God with us—God in us—God in me!

God in you!

Praise His holy, wonderful Name! For this He made us.

For this He destined us! For this He predestinated us!

For this He died and rose.

For this He sent that first mighty outpouring at Pentecost.

Praise God! Praise God!

Never stifle the cry in your heart. God put it there.

God puts no special premium on our being perennial
    spiritual Pollyannas.

His joy springs forth most abundantly

in souls that have been soaked in tears.

Not the tears of self-pity—never—

but the tears of devotion and longing for Him.

Weep. But when you weep, weep in His arms.

Doubt if you must, but candidly tell Him your doubts.

You will be surprised how quickly they will melt away.

His love and His smile will dispel every doubt

as silently and surely as sunshine removes frost.

You cannot look in His face and doubt at the same time!

You Have Run Into My Arms

Surely goodness and mercy shall follow me all the days of my life;
And I will dwell in the house of the LORD forever.

PSALM 23:6

O My child, you thought you would run from Me. But I am everywhere in front of you, and you have only run into My arms. I care for you—yes, I think of you constantly, and I seek to do you good.

You fear My rod of correction; but as it is written, it is the love of God that causes men to repent. Take My love, and in the taking, your heart shall be warmed and made tender, and at the same time encouraged and made stronger, so you will not need the rod, nor anticipate My displeasure.

For if it is true that human love covers a multitude of sins (see 1 Peter 4:8), how much more true is it of the divine love of God the Father! Knowing My deep love for you, your own heart will no longer condemn you. My mercies are everlasting, My kindness, abundant.

My grace extends to the least of My children, and My tenderness shall make you strong. I go before you daily to prepare your way, and you will be accompanied by My goodness and My mercy.

I Anticipate Your Dependence on Me

I have been crucified with Christ; it is no longer I who live, but Christ
lives in me; and the life which I now live in the flesh
I live by faith in the Son of God, who loved me
and gave Himself for me.

GALATIANS 2:20

O My child, give Me your heart, for out of it issues life. My hand is upon you, and I will keep you in all places wherever you go. I am your God, and I am your Father, and I will care for you and provide for you according to all that you need. I will be at your side, ready to help you whenever you call on Me. I am not unmindful of your needs, and My concern is for you.

You do not need to carry your own load, for I will be happy to help you carry it and to bear you up as well. You do not walk alone or meet any situation alone, for I am with you, and I will give you wisdom and strength, and My blessing shall be yours. Keep your heart set on Me and your affections on things above; for I cannot bless you unless you ask Me. And I cannot answer if you do not call. I cannot minister to you unless you come to Me.

Do not wait to feel worthy, for no one is worthy of My blessings. My grace bypasses your shortcomings, and I give to My children because they ask of Me and because I love them; I do not love one more than another. I give most liberally to those who ask the most of Me, for I love to have you depend on Me. This is why the Spirit within you cries, "Abba-Father." As your *Father,* I anticipate your dependence on Me. You may mature and outgrow your dependence on your human parents, but as My child, you will never "outgrow" your spiritual sonship, nor will I ever cast you out to rely on your own resources, not even when you become a parent. Indeed, then you will more fully appreciate My feelings toward you. You will then understand the love a father has for his child, and experience the desire to care for and provide; then you will know more fully how much I love you, how ready I am to help you, and how available I am to counsel with you and give you My support.

Heaven's resources are at your command, and you need never want, so long as I am your Shepherd. Do not think that since I know all about you, you need not bother to tell Me. It is true that I know, but you need to tell Me so that in the telling, you may experience the release of an open heart, and the fellowship of a Friend.

As you open your heart to Me, I will come to you. As you speak to Me, I will speak to you. As you reveal yourself to Me, I will reveal Myself to you. This is a law of life. There must be action to bring reaction. There must be a question to bring an answer. There must be an expression of love and confidence on the part of one person to arouse a corresponding response in another person.

Never presume My presence. Never assume that knowing your need, I will automatically supply. *Ask,* and it shall be given. *Call* upon Me, and I will answer you. *Tell* Me that you love Me, and I will make your heart know in a very real way My love for you and My nearness, and you shall never feel alone.

Welcome Me into your heart, and the more you sense My presence within you, the more you will feel at home no matter where you may be. Forget anything else, but never forget this.

Do Not Lie Dormant

But those who wait on the LORD
Shall renew their strength;
They shall mount up with wings like eagles,
They shall run and not be weary,
They shall walk and not faint.

ISAIAH 40:31

My child, I need you. Without your active help, I am hampered in My work, just as a human body is handicapped by an ineffective part, however small or insignificant. You cannot lie idle without hindering the ministry of the Church as a corporate body. You cannot move independently of My Spirit without causing damage to the harmonious working of the whole; for by My Spirit is oneness of thought and action produced. Never be dormant. Do not be slothful, neither let yourself fall asleep.

We know that the whole world lies in a death sleep in the lap of the wicked one, as an unsuspecting child napping in a death trap. Be watchful, diligent, and alert, for the time is at hand. Let the married man be ready for My call as though he were single, and let the man who is entangled in extraneous activities disengage himself; keep yourself free for the guidance and use of the Spirit of God, even as He directs you moment by moment.

My hand will be upon you, and My energy will be at your disposal, and you will partake of My joy. My peace will fortify your thought life, and I shall give health and strength to your bones. My love shall be your constant portion. I do not ask you to labor in drudgery, but the work of God is a labor of love, for God is love. As you live by the motivation of My Spirit, you will partake continually of My life and experience the comforting warmth of My love and My divine presence. For I am with you and in you—both to will and to do of My good pleasure. You may share all this; My pleasure is perpetual, but the pleasures of the world and the joys of the natural man last only for a moment.

As I have said before: This is the way, WALK in it. Do not turn to the left hand nor to the right, and I shall reveal Myself to you in a richer and fuller measure than you have known before. You shall know My resources will not and never can be exhausted. No, with your naked eye you could never begin to discover the vastness of the physical universe. My creative work in nature is but a beginning of all that I am. So how can you comprehend the love of God? The apostle Paul prayed for this, that you might know the scope of the love of God. What an area of infinitude awaits you!

So move out and move on, and you will find greater heights before you. Unknown riches await your discovery and unimagined joys your experience. Like Paul, learn to keep the physical under due and proper control so that the Spirit will not be restricted in any way; for the Spirit wars against the flesh, and the flesh is forever at enmity with the Spirit. Do not be overcome by evil, but squeeze out the unprofitable things by an abundance of good.

I am with you, and I will help you. Do not become discouraged or weary or fainthearted, and you will reap My rewards.

As Rains of Refreshing

As rains of refreshing, O Lord,
So pour out Your Spirit upon our waiting hearts.
As showers upon new-mown hay,
Send Your Spirit upon our thirsty souls.
For upon You, O God, do we wait.

Satisfy our hungering souls with Your abundance.
Yes, fill our longing hearts with Your fullness.
For in Your presence is fullness of Joy;
At Your right hand are eternal pleasures.

HEAD INTO THE WIND

Humble yourselves under the mighty hand of God,
that He may exalt you in due time.

1 PETER 5:6

O My beloved, do not be anxious concerning tomorrow. You shall encounter nothing of which I am not already aware. My mercy is concealed within every storm cloud. My grace flows beneath every crosscurrent. My wisdom has conceived a solution to every perplexity.

I have deliberately set obstacles in your path to test your prowess. I will not always cause favorable winds to blow upon your life, for then you would be at ease and would soon grow soft and dull. It is when the wind is high and the waves are threatening that you become alert and keen, and then I can strengthen your spiritual fiber.

The storm is not a thing to fear but rather to welcome. As soon as you have made the discovery that in the time of stress and strain you have the clearest revelations of Myself, You will learn to head into the wind with sheer delight.

Was this not true of the disciples? Looking out across the raging waters, what did they see? Was it not Jesus? Jesus— *coming to them!* To have had this happen only once would have been worth weathering many storms.

In the midst of the multi-heated fiery furnace, what did the three Hebrew lads see? Was it not the living form of Jesus Christ Himself having come to join them? Yes, He shone so brightly to them that His brilliance obliterated the sight of the flames!

No, you need have no fear. You need not fear the fickleness of providence—for behind whatever looks to you like utter chaos, I have a plan working for your good.

You need never fear whether I will be faithful to you, for if I have never failed anyone else, why would I fail you? You have an innumerable company of spectators cheering you from the ramparts of heaven, reminding you of what I did for them, and encouraging you that the struggle is not interminable; surprisingly soon it shall end in victory for you also—if you endure faithfully.

Do you fear the weakness within your own self? I have put it there to drive you to Myself. I may never answer your prayers to be made strong, but I *will* give you the same promise I gave the apostle Paul, that in your weakness I will be your strength. It is still true that My grace operates most effectively when you have a conscious sense of need—yes, even a desperate awareness of your own complete helplessness.

Miracles burst forth out of the moist, cold soil of human tragedy. Moist with tears and cold with hopelessness. I never get a chance to do miracles for you when you are occupied with self-realization—while you are entertaining ideas about what wonderful thing I am going to make out of *you*. I do not use *you* for material for miracles; I make miracles out of My own Being. I allow you to watch Me after you thoroughly understand that it is I who am supernatural, not you.

You do not have to be other than what I created you: human. You are only obligated to do that for which I created you: glorify Me. Stand back! Let God be God. Let man be man. Once you accept your limitations and settle the fact once and for all that I will never ask you to perform Herculean feats, you can begin to learn what I really have in mind for you.

I am not discouraged with you, but you will become discouraged with yourself if you are not able to comprehend the truth of what I taught through Paul, that it is the foolish whom I use to confound the wise, and the things which are nothing to shatter man's pride in the things he has made himself.

I *am* the Ruler, and I *will* reign. You can resist Me, but it shall inevitably be to your own destruction. Love Me and trust Me, and stay in a place of humility. Mind you, *God* will exalt you. You need not exalt yourself.

You need only stay humble.

The Mind of God

Your faith should not be in the wisdom of men but in the power of God.

1 CORINTHIANS 2:5

O My child, give Me your mind. I shall keep it in perfect tranquility. Give Me your thoughts. I will keep them in peace. If you allow other people to do your thinking for you, you will be distressed. If you try to think for yourself, you may be in error through limited knowledge or misinformation. But let the Mind of Christ be in you. Let My thinking displace and supersede your mind and your reasoning, and you will be kept in peace and order; you will know exactly and precisely what is right, what is true, and what is the proper course of action.

As you draw upon My Spirit for physical strength, draw also upon My Mind for wisdom, understanding, and peace of mind. Make this a habit in your life, and you will be astounded at the results, the accomplishments it will bring. Rather than being motivated by impulse, you will be directed by Divine Intelligence.

Have I not promised that if any of you lack wisdom, you may ask of God who gives liberally and without reproach (see James 1:5)? I have not left you to flounder like a rudderless ship. I will freely share with you all you need of My thinking powers, just as I share of My grace for the needs of the spirit.

This is a reservoir very nearly untapped. This is why I commended Solomon, because he asked the highest gift. In adding the other benefits, I gave him only those things that shall surely always follow after this first. For the life truly directed by My Mind shall enjoy many other blessings in abundance.

You shall know who needs healing, and what the physical body needs, even the true cause of illness, so that healing may be complete in the whole person. You shall know who is speaking in error, and you shall not only discern the craftiness of the enemy but how to rebuke him in My Name.

You shall be unafraid when you face others, for wisdom is power. You shall be unashamed to speak, for you shall know that the words you speak are not your own, but His Who sent you and made you His messenger. You shall be able to testify as did Jesus: "The words that I speak to you I do not speak on My own authority; but the Father who dwells in Me does the works" (John 14:10). Know that I will do it. Trust Me to do it. You will rejoice far in excess of any joy you have yet experienced.

Amazing things await you. You have had but the tiniest foretaste. Launch out! The Mind of God is fathomless. Who can ponder the smallest fraction of the intelligence of the Creator? It is all at your disposal—a great repository from which you may freely draw. Draw, then, for truly the well is deep.

I Have Planned
Ahead for You

You hold me by my right hand. You will guide me with Your counsel,

PSALM 73:23–24

Behold, am I a God that is afar off, and not a God that is near? For in the midst of difficulties, I will be your support. In the darkness, I am your Light; there is no darkness that can hide My face from the eye of faith. My beauty and My radiance are all the lovelier in darkness.

In grief, My comfort is more poignant. In failure, My encouragement the most welcome. In loneliness, the touch of My presence more tender. You are hidden in Me; and I will multiply both the wisdom and the strength in due proportion to meet the demands of every occasion.

I am the Lord your God. I know no limitations. I know no lack. I need not reserve My stores, for I always have a fresh supply. You can by no means ever exhaust My infinite resources. Let your heart run wild. Let your imagination go vagabond. No extravagance of human thought can ever plumb the depths of My planning and provision for My children.

Rejoice, therefore, and face each day with joy; for I have planned ahead for you, and made all necessary arrangements and reservations. I am your guide and benefactor. Put your hand in Mine.

DYNAMOS OF PRAISE

Everyone who asks receives, and he who seeks finds,
and to him who knocks it will be opened.

MATTHEW 7:8

O My child, lean on Me; for I am your helper; I am your shield and your buckler. Yes, I am your strong tower and support. No evil will befall you, for you are surrounded and protected by My presence, and no evil can touch Me. Yes, let your heart rejoice in Me, and occupy your heart with praise. There is no need I will not fulfill as you praise and worship—both your needs and the needs of others.

Man has contemplated the power of faith and of prayer, but only rarely have I revealed to men this far greater power of praise. Doors are opened by prayer and faith, but by praise and worship, great dynamos of power are set in motion, as when a switch is thrown and an electric power plant goes into operation. Praying for specifics is like requesting light for individual houses in various scattered places, while worshiping and praise flood the whole area with available current.

I do not discount prayer and petitions. I only show you a more marvelous way—a faster means of bringing more help to more people. So many need Me. So little time is available. Turn loose your praises, and in proportion to your liberality, you will see My generosity expressed in infinite magnitude.

Do not try to analyze each need. Leave the diagnosis and the mechanics of it in My hands. Complexities are nothing to Me. They exist only in your mind, sown by the enemy, to dull your faith. Ignore all this. Weigh nothing except the love of My heart. Ask nothing unless you ask your own heart how much love it holds for Me. Hold Me closely; never let Me go. I will bless you, and I will make you a blessing.

I will make *you* a blessing. Do not think you will *take* a blessing to someone, or hope that I will *send* a blessing. I will make you, as My ambassador, a sweet savor of life and grace. Through your saltiness others will become thirsty. Through your joy others will long for reality.

Through your peace and confidence others will seek Me, and they shall find Me even as you found Me. I will reveal Myself to them even as I revealed Myself to you—perhaps in a different way, because each has different needs, but I *will* open the door to all who knock. I *will* reward those who seek Me. *I* will reward. You need only preserve your soul's integrity. This is enough to fully occupy your energies and attention. Leave the miracles to Me. You *be* and I will *do*.

I Shall Rejoice
in My People

By My Spirit, I will have the victory.

By My Spirit, I will open the eyes of the blind;

    for surely I will move, and no hand shall stop Me.

I will break through the locked gates as a flow of flaming lava.

I will not withhold My power and My glory from any seeking

    heart.

They who desire Me, I will surely reward: I will not fail.

I will fill every longing heart and satisfy every craving soul.

    My grace will pour out as a tumbling waterfall.

    I shall be glorified, I shall be magnified,

        and I will rejoice in My people

    when they yield themselves fully and freely to Me

        and cut themselves free from everything else.

Then I shall cast My love about them as a cloak,

    and I will whisper My words in their ears.

GROW UP IN ME

The fruit of the Spirit is love, joy, peace, longsuffering, kindness,
goodness, faithfulness, gentleness, self-control.

GALATIANS 5:22–23

O My people, I have purposes for you that embrace eternity. Before the creation of the worlds, I planned for your redemption, for it is written of the Lord Jesus Christ that He was the Lamb foreordained before the foundation of the world (see 1 Peter 1:19–20). I have manifested Him to you, so that you have believed in Him and have been born again, not of corruptible seed but of incorruptible, of that which lives and abides forever.

Now that you are in Christ, you have My life abiding in you, and you have become a new creation. Grow up in Me now, so that you may develop into the full stature of men and women—even to the measure of the fullness of Christ (see Ephesians 4:13).

My purpose was not simply to bring you into My family to remain as babies or children. I am concerned with your maturity; with your growth in wisdom and knowledge of things pertaining to Myself; with the perfection of your ministry; and with the producing of the fruits of the Spirit in your life.

And so for this end, I have provided for you the *ministries* and *gifts* of My Holy Spirit. As you receive these by faith, and as you walk in these by faith, so that I am allowed to manifest Myself through you in this way, you will grow in Me, growing in grace and in your knowledge of Me. You will find the *fruits* of the Spirit will begin to appear in your life quite naturally, just as apples appear on the apple tree, though the tree takes no thought and experiences no effort or anxiety.

Commit to Me your sanctification. Bring your thoughts into captivity and let your mind be under the control of the Mind of Christ. Do not curb the impulses of the Spirit within you, nor refuse to allow Me the freedom to manifest Myself through you by means of the gifts. You may resist Me because you feel unworthy or unready to be used. This is a delusion of the mind. I do not use you when you feel prepared, but when I need you and you are yielded. When I use you, you will discover that I also work within you to edify your own heart and life.

You block the way to your own spiritual development if you hold Me back when I would minister through you (see Ephesians 4:12, 16).

Indeed, if the time should ever come that you feel ready, I would then be completely blocked by your pride and would be forced to use someone else.

WALK IN IT

Behold, I say to you,
This is the way. Walk in it.

I am the Way.
Walk in Me.
I am the truth. *Believe Me* (trust in Me).
I am the Life. *Live in Me,* and share My life with others.

For you know not what I do now,
but you will know hereafter.
(Now we see in a glass darkly, but then, face-to-face. Now our
grasp of the ways of God is incomplete, but as we move on, we
come to understand what He has been endeavoring to do in
our lives.)

Rejoice.
Rejoice not so much in victories as in the fact that I am
leading.
Praise Me.
Not so much for My blessings as for My love that prompts
them.
Serve Me with gladness,
not for the ultimate nor present reward,
but for the thrill of knowing that we labor together;
that I stand beside you in every enterprise, however trivial.

EWELS

For as the sufferings of Christ abound in us,
so our consolation also abounds through Christ.

2 CORINTHIANS 1:5

O My Bride, My Beloved:

I have betrothed you to Myself. I have given you a special token of our relationship and our future union, for I have sealed you with My precious Holy Spirit; and you will be Mine in that day when I make up My jewels. You will be as a diadem upon My brow; yes, My crowning glory.

For I will reign over kings and nations and peoples; I will rule over all the earth, but you shall have a special place of honor, for you are My prize possession. As it is written, having shared My agony, you shall that day share My glory; having borne for Me the cross, you will then share with Me the throne. (Do you know that you will even judge angels? [see 1 Corinthians 6:3])

Rejoice, now, that you have been chosen and counted worthy to suffer for My sake. We share one common destiny, and we walk one single path. The present may hold sorrow and isolation; but cheer your heart with the raptures that lie ahead. Some who live in the revelries and riches of the present world will in that day become mourners and paupers. Will you exchange places? Will you desert Me now and be rejected then? Will you ignore Me now and be rejected by Me then?

No, you will not! Rather, you will do as Paul: you will glory while suffering and in affliction, because you know they will be counterbalanced by an exceedingly greater portion of joy in that day.

✛

ℐ Joy Over You

I have no greater joy than to hear that my children walk in truth.
3 JOHN 4

My child, My little one, My under-shepherd, My dear friend: you are many things to Me, just as I am many things to you. My love for you is deep and tender. I know your desire to please Me, and I am happy that it is so. How can I tell you that though I desire holiness, and while I desire fruit in your life, still My love for you is not contingent upon anything you attain? My glory is involved in the way you live. Eternal destinies are involved in the matters of your holiness and your faithfulness and your obedience to My direction and will; but My love for you is independent of these factors.

I love you because you are My child. I love you because I am your Father. I love you with Calvary love. At a great price I redeemed you—because I have always loved you. When I planned this, I foresaw you lost in sin; and I loved you, chose you, and set My heart upon you.

Rather than struggling to comprehend the working of My sovereignty, accept this, and rejoice in it. Draw near to Me without spoiling the preciousness of our fellowship with shadows of self-condemnation.

You are Mine, and I joy over you. Discipline I reserve for the rebellious. The first step of repentance brings My mercy.

Mercy there was great, and grace was free—
Pardon there was multiplied to me,
There the burdened soul found liberty,
At Calvary.

WILLIAM R. NEWELL

Let the peace of God rule in your heart and mind, and be filled with thanksgiving.

LEARN TO REIGN

Let us continually offer the sacrifice of praise to God,
that is, the fruit of our lips,
giving thanks to His name.

HEBREWS 13:15

Call My people to repentance. Call them to their knees for prayer and fasting, for confession and vigilance—for this is a strategic hour. The enemy is rejoicing already over his anticipated victories. You can disappoint him and thwart his evil designs if you lay hold on the throne of God in steadfast, believing prayer.

Yes, you must do even as the devil has done and anticipate your victories. You can do *more* than the enemy at this point. You can claim the victories in the Name of Jesus, and all that you claim in that all-powerful Name is sealed in Heaven before it comes to pass on earth. The enemy is defeated, even before the actual battle.

Lay hold of this, My people. This is not only a glorious truth in which to rejoice, but it is *absolutely vital to your victory*. How do troops go to battle in earthly warfare? Not without preparation, ample ammunition, and intensive training. I do not expect you to meet your adversary unequipped, unarmed, or undisciplined.

Do not count on Me to deliver you by some kind of magic.

I give you orders and you must obey; otherwise you will suffer intolerable defeat. You do not face light skirmishes in which you can look for easy victories. I remind you that you are not contending with flesh and blood and matching wits with men; you are being ambushed and facing open attack from the very enemy of your souls, Satan himself.

He is not out to torment. He is out to destroy; not to hurt you, but to crush you. Your strength is no match for him. You must learn how to lay claim to the throne of God. I have met him and won already as I hung on the cross. Now YOU must find the way of victory yourselves—each one individually—so that My victory already won can become a present victory in operation for you.

Do not cry to Me in the hour of crisis and distress as though I would extend some miracle in answer to prayer. Of course, I do answer prayer, and I can perform miracles and bring deliverance, but if I do this, I have only rescued one of My own out of trouble while you have won no victory at all! I want to teach you how to circumvent the enemy—to drive him out of the arena; how to subdue kingdoms and how to truly reign in the kingdom of heaven. I want you to experience Jerichos, not Ais. You *must* be overcomers if My work is to be accomplished.

You are not qualified to be used for My purposes as long as you are being harassed by the enemy and I keep needing to rescue you from a constant parade of distressing predicaments. *You are more than conquerors*, as the apostle Paul said, and it was by My Spirit that Paul was taught this (see Romans 8:37).

Rise up, then, and lay claim to the power that is yours, because I am in you, and you are in Me, and as I was in the world, so are you. I was victorious, and you too may be victorious. I withstood every encounter with the devil, and you too can stand against him. I healed the sick and wrested tortured bodies out of the grip of evil forces, and you too can do the same.

Learn to reign, for I have made you to become kings and priests. I have intended that you should come into that place where you share My authority so I will be able to manifest My glory through you. This is My greatest joy—to lift you out of enemy territory, and seat you in the heavens with Me. And where am I? At the right hand of the Father who sits upon the throne. He has invested in Me all power in heaven and earth and under the earth; and you are seated with Me, far above all principalities and powers. Through Me you have inherited all. And you can lay claim to that inheritance now because I have already died. Because I have already died, you can enter in *now.* You do not gain an inheritance when you die, but when the testator dies. *Take it,* My people. It is yours now. It is yours because of Calvary. When you think of Calvary you think of My love; and this indeed is the tie—in between Calvary and this sharing of My throne life. I want you with Me. I want you seated beside Me because I want you near Me. Because I love you.

Where do you expect to see a queen? Beside the king. I have not spoken of you as a queen, but you are My Bride. A queen is subordinate to a king, and he reigns while she merely stands nearby. No, ours is a closer relationship, for I have vested you with authority also. You reign with Me if you recognize your privilege to do so, and if you move out in the power of the Spirit into that realm where I want you to live and move and, yes, to have your very being. For I would have a people who live in Me continually, not moving in and out of this place at will. I would have you live continually in the center of the kingdom of God, just as I have placed the Kingdom within the very center of your being. You bring this kingdom into operation in your own life by an act of faith, yes, by a constant attitude of faith.

In the last days, I will have a people through whom I can manifest My glory. There are works I must yet do through My body, the Church, which I could not possibly have accomplished through My own physical body in My earthly ministry. I am even now bringing this body together, uniting the individual members, breathing My breath into it, empowering it with gifts and ministries in order that through it I may do My work—so that when the time comes for me to take the Church out of the world, I may be able to say again, "It is finished" (John 19:30).

Know that there are also sufferings yet to be accomplished in the body of the Church that I was not able to suffer on the cross. Did Paul not write that you fill up "what is lacking in the afflictions of Christ" (Colossians 1:24)? Be patient, hold steady through the days that lie ahead, and know that the trials and suffering are working toward a consuming glory.

Praise Me, O My people, praise Me. Praise Me out of a heart full of love. Praise Me for every blessing and every victory. Yes, praise Me when the most difficult thing to do is to praise. This is the victory that overcomes the world, even your faith, and praise is the voice of faith. It is faith rejoicing for victories claimed in advance. The song of praise is made of the very fabric of things hoped for. It becomes evidence of unseen things. It is the raw material in My hands from which I fashion your victories.

Give it to Me. Give Me much. Give to Me often. I dwell in the midst of the praises of My people. I dwell there because I am happiest there. As surely as you make Me happy with your praising, you will make the enemy most unhappy. He has no power whatsoever over a praising Christian. He cannot stand against a praising Church. This is the most powerful weapon you can use against him. So praise is like a two-edged sword: one side brings health to your own spirit while the other side cuts down the enemy.

OPEN YOUR HEART TO ME

May He grant you according to your heart's desire,
And fulfill all your purpose.

PSALM 20:4

O My child, I need you for Myself. I have purposes for your life beyond your comprehension. Yes, I have truth concerning Myself to give to you that is deeper, richer, and more wonderful than your understanding has yet imagined.

Open wide your heart to Me. I will fill you with My Holy Spirit, and in so doing I will satisfy the deepest longings of your soul.

FORTITUDE

For this very reason, giving all diligence, add to your faith virtue,
to virtue knowledge, to knowledge self-control, to self-control
perseverance, to perseverance godliness, to godliness brotherly kindness,
and to brotherly kindness love. For if these things are yours
and abound, you will be neither barren nor unfruitful
in the knowledge of our Lord Jesus Christ.

2 PETER 1:5–8

Through a multitude of tests, you will learn courage. It does not matter the price you pay, but at any cost you must obtain strength of character and the fortitude to endure. I would build your resources until you are able to carry unusually heavy loads and withstand intense pressures.

You will become an ambassador of the Kingdom of Heaven to whom I can assign critical missions, confident that you are equipped to fulfill them.

It will be in vain if you anticipate resting in a comfortable place. Zion is already filled with those who are at ease. No, you will find yourself put in a place of training and discipline, so that when the moments of crisis come you will not become fainthearted, and you will not be the victim of unwonted fear.

Trust My instruction in all of this, as you have in various past experiences. I am faithful and loving, and I am doing this so that you may meet the future days, and not be found wanting.

On Doing
the Father's Work

Every tree is known by its own fruit.
For men do not gather figs from thorns,
nor do they gather grapes from a bramble bush.

LUKE 6:44

Behold, there is a day coming when you will regret your lethargy, and you will ask, "Why did we leave the vineyard of the Lord untended?" Those things that have occupied you will appear for what they are—chaff and worthlessness. For there will be nothing of lasting value, and no reward for the works of your hands which you have done in your own strength, and which I have not commanded you to do.

Jesus Himself was directed by the Father in all that He said and did. Dare you live according to the dictates of your own human heart and puny human understanding?

I have fashioned you for better things. Do not fail Me. Place your life under My divine control and learn to live in the full blessing of My highest will.

I will strengthen you and comfort you; I will lead you by the hand.

LISTEN TO THE SILENCE

For with God nothing will be impossible.

LUKE 1:37

Find Solitude

Now therefore, listen to me, my children,
For blessed are those who keep my ways.

PROVERBS 8:32

There is no blessing I would withhold from those who walk in obedience to Me—who follow when I call, who respond when I speak to them. Near to My heart and precious in My sight are those who have eyes to discern My purpose and ears that listen to My direction.

Do not be intent on great accomplishments. By what standards do you judge the importance of a matter? It was a relatively small thing that Hannah prayed for a son, but what great things I accomplished through Samuel! It may have seemed incidental that Simeon and Anna perceived the Christ Child and prophesied over Him; but for Me it was an event worthy to be recorded in Holy Scripture and preserved forever (see Luke 2:25–38).

No, you cannot ascertain the ways of God amid the pathways of men. You may feel the wind as I pass and yet see only the swirling dust. The earthly obscures the heavenly. Human voices drown out the voice of God. Only in solitude can you begin to sift away the chaff and come at last to the golden grains of truth.

The world will confuse you. Silence will speak more to you in a day than the world of voices can teach you in a lifetime. Find silence. Find solitude—and having discovered her riches, bind her to your heart.

*B*E MY ALLY

And [Jesus] said to them,
"Come aside by yourselves to a deserted place and rest a while."

MARK 6:31

My children, do not fear nor resist My voice. When I speak to you, you will know that it is I, the Lord God. As I spoke to Isaiah I will speak to you. Is it not strange that you are astonished at the way I speak to you? Instead, those who do *not* hear My voice ought to marvel!

Never be distressed by those who doubt the way I deal with you. Instead, pray that the same blessed privilege will be granted to them: that their ears be unstopped, and their spirits become sensitive and receptive to the ministering of My Holy Spirit. Pray they may be given a hunger and a burning desire to fellowship more closely with Me.

There is no food for the soul nor ease for the heart in an intellectual religion, in outward forms and fleshly service. These, while not evil in themselves, are to the soul, as the Bible declares, only filthy rags; and this is no fit nourishment for the soul.

When I promised you green pastures, I did not have religious activity in mind. When I said, "Come, buy wine and milk without money and without price" (Isaiah 55:1), I was not challenging you to fevered service but to contemplative fellowship and collective communion. Only thus are souls made strong, hearts made pure, and minds refreshed.

Your busyness wearies Me. Small wonder you are yourself fatigued! Your fretfulness grieves Me. I long to take it from you and give you instead the balm of Gilead. *Be My ally.* I will endow you with life so dynamic that you will serve Me before you have time to even think about putting forth the effort to do so. . . .

STAY PLIABLE
IN MY HAND

The thief does not come except to steal,
and to kill, and to destroy.
I have come that they may have life,
and that they may have it more abundantly.

JOHN 10:10

O My child, be quick to obey. For the moving of My Spirit may at times be inconvenient to the flesh, and may at other times be diametrically opposed to reason, but obey Me regardless of the cost. You will always be amply repaid for any sacrifice with an abundance of blessing. The more difficult the assignment, the richer the reward.

I will not force you to make the choice, nor make My will inescapable. There will always be an easier way open to you and, to your mind, one that will seem more reasonable, involving less risk. I have calculated the risk to test and develop your faith as well as your obedience, and in the choosing process, I give you an opportunity to prove your love for Me.

Be sensitive to My Spirit. Be listening for My voice. I will guide you with My hand upon your shoulder. I do not intend to circumscribe your way nor handicap your freedom, but I intend to lead you into an increasingly abundant life, and by crucifying the desires of the flesh, to liberate your spirit.

Stay pliable in My hand; don't resist Me or be unaware of My working; don't question what I am making. Trust and give Me a free hand. It will be a joyful surprise when the end is revealed.

I MUST HAVE OVERCOMERS

I have been crucified with Christ;
it is no longer I who live,
but Christ lives in me;
and the life which I now live in the flesh
I live by faith in the Son of God,
who loved me and gave Himself for me.

GALATIANS 2:20

O My children, the path where I will lead you is not easy for your human nature to bear. It is not a pleasant way, nor in accord with your selfish desires. I do not intend to please the self-life; instead, I will bring it to the crucifixion; for it can only be a hindrance to your spiritual progress and My working through you.

You have faith in Me; this is good, but faith without works is dead. Faith I can give you as a gift, but the works I can do through you only when your ego moves out of the way. For they are not your works, but My works, just as Jesus said, "I must work the works of Him who sent Me" (John 9:4).

Like a flood, I will cause the tears to flow through you, and I will purge out your self-life, and I will give you My love. With My love, I will give you My power; then you will no longer walk in your own way, but you will reign with Me on the throne life.

I must have overcomers through whom I may overcome. There is an enemy to be contested and defeated; and to do this, there must be more than resolve in your heart—there must be power. This power cannot operate until your self-will is out of the way. Yes, My new life will become yours in direct proportion to your success in emptying your heart of self-will.

I know you cannot do this for yourself; but you must will it to be done. And as you will it, I will work with you and within you to bring it to pass. You will know joy as never before, and as never possible any other way. You will have rest from inner conflict; yes, you must be delivered from the inner conflict in order to engage in the outer conflict with the enemy.

RENEW YOUR VOWS

At that day you will know that I am in My Father,
and you in Me, and I in you.
He who has My commandments and keeps them,
it is he who loves Me.
And he who loves Me will be loved by My Father,
and I will love him and manifest Myself to him.

JOHN 14:20–21

There is a day coming when you will say, "I have waited in vain for the Lord." You will wait for Me to speak, and you will hear only the whistling of the wind. But I tell you now, I am never silent; you are deaf. I am always speaking; but I do not find your ear attuned to listen.

You will sit alone in a desolate place and grieve in your loneliness; but it will not be that I have left you, but that you have become insensitive to My presence. Yes, if you ignore My personal nearness and fellowship and if you do not return My overtures, your perceptions will become dull; you will not be able to discern Me even though I am near at hand—even though My love for you is still as strong as before.

Do not be lukewarm, lest you be among those who are cast out of My fellowship. "How shall we escape," it is written, "if we neglect so great a salvation?" (Hebrews 2:3) But I ask you now: How will you survive in your private walk in the Spirit if you pay but faint heed to My nearness and do not respond in kind to the affection I offer you?

You will not be able to meet the needs of others with anything short of this. There is no cure for the ills of humankind but what is contained in the love of God. You cannot give to them until after you have taken it from Me.

"I will not leave you orphans" (John 14:18). It is the intention of My heart to fellowship with you closely. I am turned away by your unresponsiveness; by your preoccupation with things and with people; by your thoughtlessness and indifference.

Some have lost Me by the sin of rebellion; but I warn you that you may lose Me by the subtle way of simple inattention. Confess your coldness, and draw near to Me; and I will make My personal presence real to you again. I will hold you close to My heart, and you will hear My voice.

Renew your vows, and I will revive your ministry. There is a life ahead for you into which you could not have entered before. There is a work ready for you, and I have prepared you for it. It is too wonderful to miss. It will be silent but powerful.

I will cause the veil to drop, and you will enter a new area of experience. You will be given knowledge in My Spirit that is not to be found in books. I will share with you My thoughts, and who can tell the sum of them? You will partake of the Mind of Christ and of the Holy Spirit of God. His eyes go throughout the whole earth seeking out the thoughts and intents of the hearts of men.

You will serve Me in ways you have never heard of before. It is My work. I have laid it out for you. Keep clear of man's work. Stay free to do Mine. You will not miss it if you keep close to Me and stay sensitive to My Spirit.

No one else can do what I have reserved for you; and be very sure that if you fail, it will remain undone. Crucify the flesh, and let the Spirit thrive. Redeem the time, for surely these days abound with evil.

Bless Me. I will bless you.

THE ROAD IS STEEP

Narrow is the gate and difficult
is the way which leads to life,
and there are few who find it.

MATTHEW 7:14

You are a chosen vessel to Me, so do not be filled with filthy lucre. Be undefiled by the lusts of the flesh and untarnished by the pride of life. Be wholesome, humble, simple; for simplicity and a spirit of humility befit one who serves the Lord.

Pride lifts up. It exalts self rather than Christ. Humility brings down to the level of service, and you are not to be worshiped, but to serve.

You are My treasure. I delight in you when, and only when, you are fully yielded to Me with no thoughts of personal ambition or achievement. If you wish for anything, wish for more of My nearness. If you long after anything, long after more of My righteousness and more of My love. I will not occupy second place, and My Spirit will leave an impure vessel. Just as sin has no place in heaven, I will not dwell in peace in a heart that harbors evil.

So put away all that defiles you, just as you would cast away an evil-smelling, filthy rag. Teach others as well how to maintain mental wholesomeness, and how to experience inner cleansing through confession and rejection of all that offends the Holy Spirit.

Tolerate nothing that dulls the perception of My presence. Cut off, purge out, plead the blood of Christ, use every avenue available to you to rid your soul of sin. Never be satisfied with half measures. Never be deterred by satisfaction with the progress already achieved. Know that this is only a beginning.

Holiness is arrived at by no low road. The road to holiness is narrow and steep and exceedingly lonely. There is no other road.

"It is the way the Master went,

Shall not His servants tread it still?"

I Will Use but Not Destroy You

So shall My word be that goes forth from My mouth;
It shall not return to Me void,
But it shall accomplish what I please,
And it shall prosper in the thing for which I sent it.

ISAIAH 55:11

O My child, do not be overcharged with the cares of everyday living, and do not let your energies be consumed by humdrum tasks. What is needed, must be done; but if you put the ministry of the Kingdom in first place, My strength will be yours for other tasks, and time will be given to you for both.

You do not need to respond to every call. Learn to discern when I would use you, and when I would have the other individual lean wholly upon Me. Otherwise, you may restrict the development of the other person's spiritual ministry, and rather than helping, you may become an actual hindrance.

I will not overtax you. *I will use you, but I will not destroy you in the using.* But you may destroy yourself if you lack this discernment and fail to know when to direct others to look to Me. You fear to fail Me. You can perhaps fail Me more by attempting to help another than by refusing, if by refusing you encourage another to seek My face—My help—My instruction.

You are also in danger of giving incorrect information. You

may confuse rather than clarify the issue. Do not be used by others as a source of information, but challenge others to seek for light from the same source as you have received it. Do not try to be a substitute for My Word—either written or by prophetic message. Let the question be used as a challenge to Bible study and prayer, and be very reluctant to become the transmitter of quick learning. This poses innumerable disadvantages both for yourself and the person seeking help. Teach him how to establish communication personally with his God, so that he may "hear from heaven" himself—this is the greatest blessing you can ever give to another human being.

To be sought after for wisdom is flattering to the ego. Recognize this snare, and be on your guard against it, and bring the flesh to quick crucifixion. Do not be used as a substitute for God to anyone. Be a channel for the ministries of My Spirit, but never be a free giver of advice. Curb the impulse. Give to the other the source of your knowledge—even the Scripture passage where the answer may be found—so that My Word is constantly the first and the final authority.

I will honor My Word, and I will honor those who give My Word the sacred preeminence it deserves. My Word shall never return void. It shall accomplish My purposes.

$\mathcal{K}$EEP YOUR CHANNEL CLEAR

Whoever drinks of the water that I shall give him will never thirst.
But the water that I shall give him
will become in him a fountain of water
springing up into everlasting life.

JOHN 4:14

O My daughter, will I speak to you as one whose voice is lost in the noise of the crashing surf? Or as one who calls in vain in the midst of a deep forest, where there is no ear to hear nor voice to respond? Will you be like an instrument with broken strings from which the musician can bring forth no music?

No, I would have you be as the waterfall whose sound is continuous, as a great river whose flow is not interrupted. You shall not sing for a time and then be silent for a season. You shall not praise for a day and then revert to the current topics of everyday life.

You will never exhaust My supply. The more you give, the more shall be given to you. You are in a learning process. I have much to share with you; yes, out of the abundance of My heart I will instruct you. I want to teach you truths of heavenly wisdom which you cannot learn from human lips. I will instruct you in the way that you shall go. From whom else can you inquire?

I will bring My love and My life to you. From where else

have you any such comfort and strength? The more often you come to Me to draw of this water of Life, the more your life will be enriched in wisdom—yes, but also in many other ways. You need My grace so that you may share My truth with a right spirit. You need to keep your channel straight and clear, that My blessing is not hindered as it flows through you, and that the waters may be kept pure.

You do not indicate presumption by continually seeking My face. Rather, You show a tendency to trust in the strength of the flesh when you do not come to Me for a gift. Or have you mistakenly thought that your own mind had become a source of wisdom?

Beware of the snare of flattery, and beware even of well-intended praise. Take no glory to yourself, nor compliment yourself in your achievement. I control the waters. I gathered them up in My fist to allow the passage of the children of Israel. I flung them forth to drown the Egyptian army. I send forth the river of life now to refresh and bring life to those who thirst after Me. I dry up the streams of inspiration before the feet of the proud. Those who glory in their own thoughts shall not drink. Those who pursue the paths of human reason shall be as a desert.

I am not to be found there—as I was not found in the wind nor in the earthquake. These were natural forces. I was in the still small voice. I Myself am the direct source and the only source of eternal life. Every other well is dry. Every other pursuit is vain.

But you shall be a fountain flowing forth whose streams shall not fail, for I, the Lord your God, dwell in the midst of you.

✙

SPEAK THE TRUTH

Finally, my brethren, be strong in the Lord
and in the power of His might.

EPHESIANS 6:10

Do not be intimidated by anyone, but speak forth My Word as I give it to you. You have written freely and fearlessly. Now speak in the same way. Your spoken word must be brought into conformity with the work I have done within you. This you need for your own personal sense of unity. This you need for your own strength. For the house divided against itself cannot stand; neither can you so long as you bear one testimony in your heart and another with your lips.

You are not pleasing Me but trying to please men. They will detect your inconsistency in spite of your best efforts, for in one way or another, the truth will break through. You need not say all that is in your heart, but you must either speak the truth or be silent. If you cannot bring yourself to speak the truth without apology, then speak nothing.

Let the life and witness of Jesus Christ be your guide. If you are willing to attempt to emulate His honesty, I will come to your aid to give you the wisdom also; so that the answer may be not only true but forceful. For you wrestle not against flesh and blood, but against the unseen opposition of satanic forces. These may at times be arrayed against your soul even through your dearest friends, so that you may have to reply as Jesus did to Peter on one occasion (see Mark 8:33).

Do not set out to convert the world to your convictions but rather to hold your own convictions inviolable against the forces of the opposition. I will be with you, and will guard your mouth. Trust Me.

COME AWAY, MY BELOVED

Come out from among them
And be separate, says the Lord.

2 CORINTHIANS 6:17

My beloved, you do not need to make your path, for I go before you. Yes, I will engineer circumstances on your behalf. I am your husband; I will protect you, care for you, and make full provision for you.

I know your need, and I am concerned for you: for your peace, for your health, for your strength. I cannot use a tired body, and you need to take time to renew your energies, both spiritual and physical. I am the God of battle, but I am also the One who said, "Those who wait on the LORD shall renew their strength" (Isaiah 40:31).

I will teach you, as I taught Moses on the back side of the desert, and as I taught Paul in Arabia. In the same way, I will teach you, and it will be a constructive period, not in any sense wasted time. Like the summer course to the schoolteacher, it is vital to you in order to become fully qualified for your ministry.

There is no virtue in activity in and of itself—nor in inactivity. I minister to you in solitude that you may minister Me to others as a spontaneous overflow of our communion. Never labor to serve, nor force opportunities. Set your heart to be at peace and to sit at My feet. Learn to be ready but not to be anxious. Learn to say "no" to human demands and to say "yes" to the call of the Spirit. These may sometimes be at variance. Do not be distressed by the misunderstanding of people. Let Me take care of them Myself. They too must learn this same important lesson, and you can help them by setting the example; but if you try to please them by answering every demand, you will both fall into the same snare.

I am a jealous God, and I am always at peace with Myself. I would have you also to be at peace with My Spirit within you. As you give Me My rightful place and do not allow others to intrude, you will be at peace with Me. Be very serious in this. I am not speaking to you lightly. I was never more earnest in any message I have brought to you. Do not fail Me. I have brought you this message at various times in the past. It was never more urgent than now.

For people are experiencing a new awakening, and they are searching for My Truth more than ever. I must speak through My prophets; and if they are not set apart for Me, how can I instruct them? Yes, I will nourish you by the brook as I nourished Elijah; and I will speak to you out of the bush as I spoke to Moses, and reveal My glory on the hillside as I did to the shepherds.

Come away, My beloved; be like the doe on the mountains; and we will go down together to the gardens.

Take the Glory with You

Not holding fast to the Head, from whom all the body,
nourished and knit together by joints and ligaments,
grows with the increase that is from God.

COLOSSIANS 2:19

Behold, I have brought you out of a dark and solitary land. I have given you a drink from My own hand. We have held sweet counsel together; for I have not called you servant, but I have called you friend. Yes, and I delight in your companionship. For I have seen your devotion, and I have observed with pleasure your thoughtfulness to those less fortunate who have crossed your path.

When you have encouraged the weary; prayed with the sick; lent help to the needy, comfort to the sorrowing, and understanding to the distressed, I count it as though you did it for Me, for I know that except for your deep love for Me, you would not make this kind of sacrifice.

Gifts may be given, prompted by many a selfish motive; but when you give yourself, often in the face of insults, returning good for evil, and yet receive further censure, this I know you have done because and only because you love Me first, and loving Me you find no place to hate any. For if a man loves God, truly he will also love his brother. And he will yet go beyond this, for he will show kindness and feel concern for the needs of even his enemies, and be moved with compassion to minister aid.

Did I not say that we must go into the valley together? I have given you the enjoyment of My fellowship on the mountaintop to prepare you for the ministry in the valley of service. *Take the glory of the mountaintop with you;* take My presence, My light, My love. This is not the valley of personal darkness—this is the valley where you will find those who need the touch of blessing you can bring.

And I am with you, yes, more so than in any other kind of valley; for in this we are one in a very special way. For the Son of Man came to seek and to save the lost; to seek the lost, to lift the fallen, and to heal the bruised.

As you minister together with Me to those in need, you fill up that which is left of the sufferings of Christ (see Colossians 1:24). My physical sufferings—the broken body, the shed blood, My death—these were completed at the cross. But the travail of soul until the completion and perfection of the Body of Christ, this continues until My coming in power and glory to receive My chosen Bride.

(For I have chosen each member of the body as an individual, and the Church as a corporate body—so you are twice chosen—individually, and collectively.)

So as you "pour out your soul," you share with Me in My

travail until the completion of the purchased possession; until you all come through the power of the Spirit into the full stature of the Body of Christ, growing up together in Him, each part developing through the nourishment each joint supplies. By mutual nurture and encouragement you stimulate growth in each other.

Only as you yield individually can the work be accomplished. One member in rebellion or hostility slows the growth and injures the health of those about him.

So yield yourself to the moving of the Spirit in your heart, and minister as I arrange your contacts, without looking around to make your own choices. Leave the planning to the Head. This is My work. Let each abide in his place, yielding completely to My Spirit, nourished by My love, and ministering in self-sacrifice.

LISTEN TO THE SILENCE

He who dwells in the secret place of the Most High
Shall abide under the shadow of the Almighty.

PSALM 91:1

You are in My hands. You are not keeping yourself; I am keeping you. If I choose to hide you away, it is for a reason. If I wish to give you a time of rest, it is for your own good. Nothing is amiss that is in My will. Do not think that it will be as times in the past. I have deeper lessons to teach you. How invaluable have you found the truths to be that I taught you in your "Arabia years." But Arabia was not the only solitary period in the life of My apostle, Paul. Indeed, it was rather insignificant in comparison to the later prison-day experiences.

One does not write what has already been written. One writes out of the storehouse of fresh revelation and personal knowledge gained through the painful experiences of growth. You cannot escape the growing experience without forfeiting the other. You will cease writing if you cease learning. You do not learn as you write, but write as you learn.

I would spare you if I could do so in love; but this kind of protecting love would be false, and would rob you of much treasure. I only love you truly as I give you My best. My best cannot come to you without pain, even as it could not come to the Lord Jesus without pain. Pain is the result of sin, true; and sin is still an existing problem with which to be dealt. It must be grappled with. Empires do not simply fall, but are taken by a stronger force. The kingdom of Satan must likewise be opposed by a stronger force if you hope to see it fall.

I want to make you strong. I want you to be a Devastator. I have brought you to this place. Make the most of it. Drink in the silence. Seek solitude. *Listen to the silence.* It will teach you. It will build strength. Let others share it with you. It is priceless. It is little to be found elsewhere.

A More Glorious Way

Eye has not seen, nor ear heard,
Nor have entered into the heart of man
The things which God has prepared for those who love Him.

1 CORINTHIANS 2:9

Y ou have read that "the letter kills, but the Spirit gives life"
(2 Corinthians 3:6). I have a deeper revelation of this truth to
give you if you can receive it. For the Spirit operates in a different realm than the Word. The Word deals with you on the
plane of your everyday living. It governs your conduct in daily
affairs. It guides you into the knowledge of the doctrines of
God, the understanding of My divine will, and instructs you in
the walk of the Christian.

But in the Spirit, there is a life awaiting that would draw
you out beyond the confines of the natural world. The Spirit of
God operates in the realm of the supernatural and the infinite.

Do not hold back in wonder and disbelief. Accept My life
in the Spirit *as it is.* Do not require Me to operate within the
limitations of *your* life. I am calling you to give My Spirit
within you the liberty to move out into the dimensions of the
infinite.

Breathtaking? Perhaps. But how could you expect anything
less of Me? Push open the door. In the dazzling light of My
presence you will see much that is now obscure to you because

you have chosen to walk in the darkness. I have better things for you—things in keeping with Myself. You have not truly known Me. You have been hindered in your comprehension by what you have read and been taught. There is very little more concerning Me that you can learn from human sources. You can know Me in the Spirit only when you go deeper in your worship. I am not found in textbooks but in sanctuaries. You are not changed by knowledge but by love. Only the heart that is melted in devotion is pliable in My hand. Only the mind that is open to the Spirit can receive divine revelation.

Labor not to be wise but to be yielded, and in your attitude of submission to My Spirit I will instruct you in My truth. There will be death and there will be a glorious resurrection. The letter will convict of sin and prune away the old fallen nature, and the Spirit will bring forth within you a life that will never die. It will have faculties of perception not to be compared with the physical senses, for the mind of the Spirit is the Mind of Christ.

It shall increase and develop as you move on into God, and you will leave behind religious intellectualism and discover a more glorious way.

I Want to Do a
Beautiful Work

*. . .He is a chosen vessel of Mine
to bear My name. . . .*

ACTS 9:15

Y ou are *Mine*. You are not your own. With a great price I have purchased you for Myself. I am not dismayed that you do not comprehend, but I say that if you will listen to Me, I will reveal to you more fully so that you may know more clearly how vital you are to My purpose. There is work to be done, and I need you as a vessel through which to work. Not a vassal, but a vessel. I want to do a beautiful work.

I need an individual to use who is not only available and suitable, but who loves Me in such a way as to enhance My creation. I desire not the kind of loyalty a soldier gives to his country, but a dedicated devotion of the type of love a mother feels toward her unborn child.

There will be inconveniences to be born, self-pleasing to be laid aside, sacrifices and pain—but what a blessed reward I have in store! Yes, in store for *you,* if you are able to let Me use you the way I desire.

You are not unworthy; you are not unprepared. You have no reason to hold back unless your love for Me is too small. If this is the only hindrance, draw closer to Me, and I will pour My love out upon you so that your affection for Me may be deepened and perfected. Lo, I wait for you. Come to Me.

⁙

Jhe Secret of Silence (Praise and Reproof)

Behold, you are fair, my love!
Behold, you are fair!
SONG OF SOLOMON 1:15

My child, do not let the words of others influence you unduly—neither their praise nor their criticism. Weigh each for its proper value, and come back to Me again. Only in communion with Me can you be sure of the truth. If I correct you, you know it is for your betterment. If I encourage you with a word of praise, it is because I know you need it; so rejoice in it and accept it as wholeheartedly as you accept My rebukes.

You know My rebukes are for your benefit. Can you not believe that My words of commendation are for the same purpose? Some of your faults and weaknesses can best be helped and corrected by *praise* rather than by *reproof*. When you turn a deaf ear in an effort to be humble, you are not helping. You cannot be truly humble until you have a deep sense of being loved.

Knowing and truly feeling that such great love is not merited in the face of your many imperfections will generate more honest humility than a thousand rebukes for obvious failures. You are condemned already by your own heart. There is a subtle pride that seeks to hide these glaring imperfections in the effort to hold some vestige of self-esteem and invoke the respect of others. This is a craftiness of the enemy.

If you will accept My love and My approval, you will be given courage to face your sins and faults so you can deal with them more decisively. The more you find of the truth about your own self, the more you will be set free. . .free from improper evaluations of your worth, free from false pride that seeks to cover recognized flaws.

I want your life, character, and personality to be as beautiful and lovely as I visualized you to be when I created you. Much has not developed perfectly. Some early beauty has been marred. *Live close to Me,* and let Me remold and re-create until I see in you the image of all I want you to be.

I love you, My child—My very dear and special child. Through your childhood years I walked very close to you, and in your childlike way you were very conscious of My presence and reality. You have made an arduous journey. You have climbed many mountains that you could easily have walked around. You have not chosen the pleasant path nor sought joys though they were readily accessible.

You have often misconstrued My will and felt that only in sacrifice and suffering could you please Me, while much of the time I have longed to deliver you out of the very pains you inflicted upon yourself. You meant to please Me, but in truth you were only marring your own beauty which is precious to Me.

I cannot rejoice in a blighted rose. You have gone far enough in this way. I offer you My path now, if you are strong enough to accept it. Life, liberty, love, and joy. Health and peace—simplicity and rest. It has been there for you all along. You can have it even now if you will.

I do not want you to work for Me under pressure and tension like a machine—striving to produce, produce. I only want you to live with Me as a *person*. I have waited for you to wear yourself out. I knew you would find it eventually—the secret of silence and rest, of solitude and of song.

I will rebuild your strength—not to work again in foolish frenzy, but just for the sake of making you strong and well. To Me this is an end in itself. Make it your aim and join with Me wholeheartedly in the project. Many joys are waiting yet.

The Love Covenant

All the paths of the LORD are mercy and truth,
To such as keep His covenant. . . .

PSALM 25:10

My children, there is no good thing that I would withhold from you. I have not left you to fend for yourselves nor to make your way by your own devices. I am the Lord your God. I am your provider and your defender. I care for you with a deep and tender love. I am all-wise and all-powerful, and will be your defense against every onslaught of the enemy.

Anticipate My help. I will not fail you. Look down at the path before you. You will see the print of My feet. "I will go before you and make the crooked places straight" (Isaiah 45:2). I will make the path ready for you as you follow.

It is a joy to My heart when My children rely on Me. I delight in working things out for you, but I delight even more in you yourself than in anything I do to help you. Even so, I want you to delight in Me just for Myself, rather than in anything you do for Me.

Service is the salvage of love. It is like the twelve baskets of bread that were left over. The bread that was eaten was like fellowship mutually given; and the excess and overflow was a symbol of service. I do not expect you to give to others until you have first eaten. I will provide you with plentiful supply to *give* if you first come to *receive* for your own needs.

This is not selfishness. It is the Law of Life. Can the stalk of corn produce the ear unless first it receives its own life from the parent seed? No more can you produce fruit in your ministry unless you are impregnated with divine life from its source in God Himself. It was from the hands of the Christ that the multitudes received bread. From His hands you also must receive your nurture, the Bread of Life to sustain your health and your life.

This is His love-covenant with you. It is the message of John 15:4: "Abide in Me, and I in you. As the branch cannot bear fruit of itself, unless it abides in the vine, neither can you, unless you abide in Me." This abiding is a love relationship, and this is why service is the salvage of love.

Service will be futile and burdensome unless it springs from an overflowing heart. Overflowing not with good intentions and condescending self-righteousness, but overflowing with the love of God. This you do not have of yourself, nor can you give, however much you might desire to do so. You will possess this love only as you wait upon Me and take time to absorb it from Me, like a quiet flower takes life from the warm rays of the sun.

Your heart will be cold otherwise. For your ready ardor and natural sympathy, and common kindness will soon be cooled by the chill winds of ingratitude and others' unlovely reactions. Do you think the love of Jesus was always well received? Would He not have brought His ministry to an abrupt end on many an occasion if He had needed the appreciation of people to motivate His loving service?

Have you read the reaction of the religious people to the recital of His miracle-working power in Luke 4? The exhibition of God's love draws forth emotions in the unregenerate heart that are nothing short of murderous at times. In other cases, God's love is met by callous indifference and criminal ingratitude, as with the nine lepers who never returned to express so much as a word of thanks for their deliverance from a walking death (see Luke 17:12–19).

In the face of divine love being poured forth on Calvary— the holy, sinless God Himself dying for sinful, depraved, undeserving humanity—what is the reaction? Gratitude? Love? Contrition? No! Hate lashes out in jeers and mocking. Violence and cruelty flow forth like a river and mingle with the very blood that was spilt for their redemption!

No. Human kindness will never be enough. It will never fill the twelve baskets with fragments. There will never be any crumbs left over for others unless you first eat from your own personal love feast with the Savior.

Let Him fully satisfy your soul-hunger, and then you will go forth with a full basket on your arm. Twelve baskets there were (see Matthew 14:20). One for each disciple. There will always be the multitudes to be fed, but the few called to minister. This is by My own arrangement. As the Scripture says: "My brethren, let not many of you become teachers, knowing that we shall receive a stricter judgment" (James 3:1–2).

Many are called. Few are chosen.

⁜

You Shall Move Swiftly

Be anxious for nothing, but in everything by prayer and supplication, with thanksgiving, let your requests be made known to God.

PHILIPPIANS 4:6

Behold, out of gross darkness, a light will shine. Out of the night a cry will be heard. For I will make My will known to you, and you will no longer move haltingly, *you shall move swiftly and surely*. You may not know what I am doing as yet, but you will know hereafter, and you will be moved by My divine unction and authority.

You will not be left to falter as a blind man searches out his way; with your hand in Mine, we will move together. My Spirit will be apparent by your life and testimony, and you will be empowered by My might and power.

My strength never fails. Yes, I will be to you an energizing and a quickening power within you and upon you, and you will go in the strength of your God. You will not fail; nor will your arm droop nor your foot lag.

You have no enemy to fear but only fear itself. You have no weakness to contend with but that which doubt may produce. Look to Me; yes, constantly set your eyes upon My face, and you will be as the eagle and as the deer. Rest your heart in Me. For in quietness and in returning shall be your peace and your strength.

Be anxious for nothing, but in all situations in prayer and in fasting, bring each emergency case to Me, for I am the Great Physician; many are the afflictions of the righteous, but the Lord heals them all.

Blessings, honor, praise, and glory be to God forever and ever. Amen.

The Gift of Forgiveness

Launch out into the deep and let down your nets for a catch.

LUKE 5:4

O My child, come to Me—I want to give you a new gift. I want you to see all people as being under the shed sacrifice of the blood of Christ.

He has died for all. His forgiveness encompasses all. Tell them. It is the Good News. They will accept it even as they have received eagerly and joyfully the message of My love. It is the confidence in your own heart that will engender faith to receive within the hearts of others.

Freely forgive all, as you have freely loved all. Those to whom you extend My forgiveness will come to experience it for themselves. It is like extending a helping hand to lift another across a brook. Having gained the safety of the other side, he needs your help no longer but stands as secure as your-self; but he needed assistance in crossing over.

Do not be dull and slow. Many are waiting for an outstretched hand. Many have hung a black veil of self-condemnation between their guilty hearts and the light and power of My forgiveness. You can approach them from the other side and reach them with the message where they have no preset defense.

They are all around you. Sing My love, shout it, speak it patiently, and whisper it tenderly. The dead will rise to life; the hopeless to joy; the despondent to courage; the poor to receive My bounty.

The sins you forgive will be forgiven. Those who receive no ministry may never find their way through to the light, not knowing the path. The mysteries of the Kingdom have been committed and entrusted to you. Do not store them away in hidden vaults. Scatter them along your way and place the jewels in the empty hands of those you encounter on the road of life.

You will find the Christ Himself standing beside you, and you will see His smile. You may have only a small place in the life of your brother, but you will have a very special place in the heart of your Lord. Go, then, in faith, giving My forgiveness. Blessings shall attend you, and heaven will rejoice in your successes.

I am bringing you into a new ministry. The former shall be enriched and made more full and more meaningful. I am not undoing anything. I am adding. I shall be enriching your own soul and bring about your sanctification.

You need many graces as well as many gifts. The *graces* of your soul accompany you into the next life, whereas the *gifts* are left behind. For this reason the health of your soul is of more importance than the fullness of your ministry. But each time you launch out into a new ministry you bring new life and strength and health-building forces into operation within your own soul.

⊹

THE EYE OF THE SPIRIT

I have led you in right paths.
When you walk, your steps will not be hindered,
And when you run, you will not stumble.

PROVERBS 4:11–12

O My children, I am the door. I am the door of salvation. I am the door of peace and hope. Yes, I am the door of revelation. And just as My written Word is the revelation of the Lord Jesus Christ, so will My spoken word be to you. It will be an unveiling before your very eyes of the person and the work of the Anointed One. For you will not be as those who remain to this day with a veil over their eyes.

No, you will be like My servant, the apostle Paul, who in his baptism experience had the scales fall from his eyes, and what visions were given to him in the Spirit! You too shall see. You shall *see,* for the Lord your God will grant to you foresight and insight, and you will be allowed to look into those things Scripture says are hidden even from the angels.

You will see the coming together of the Body of Christ. You will behold the glory. You will see visions of things to come, and of some you will witness the fulfillment. You shall be given discernment. Yes, that which is in darkness will be as though it were exposed to light; yes, that which is hidden will be revealed to you. For in the eye of the Spirit there is no darkness, and you will see with the eye of the Spirit.

The limitations of your natural vision will be no handicap. The Spirit is not detained by the flesh. The Spirit will move in spite of the flesh, and will accomplish a renewal and do a work of re-creating, so that the newly liberated creature will rise up in virgin life, starting out upon a ministry the foundations of which no man has laid. It will be a path of holiness, a way of miracles, and a life of glory. You will see My shining smile.

Nothing will be required of you but obedience. You will follow the call of the Spirit and not search for the path; for the way will be laid down before you as you tread. Wherever you stop, there will the path stop also. Whenever you walk in faith, the way will be made clear before you.

Be as a young child and step out in confidence, knowing that with your hand in Mine you will be always safe, and blessings will attend you.

My Kingdom Is at Hand

Fear God and give glory to Him, for the hour of His judgment has come;
and worship Him who made heaven and earth,
the sea and springs of water.

REVELATION 14:7

By My Spirit, I will speak to My people. Those who hear My voice will sing of My glory. Those who behold My countenance will be filled with rejoicing. They will bring their offerings of praise, and I will bless them out of the riches of My heart. The more they bless Me, the more will I honor them. Those who are pure of heart will walk in a path of delight. Joy is the natural climate of heaven, and My chosen ones—who delight in Me—will have a full portion even now.

Be prepared for Me, for I will come to you in blinding splendor, and you will not be able to bear it if you have been regarding the darkness about you. Look above the present scene, for to dwell on the confusion of the world would render you unfit for the revelation of heaven. You are not going to be here much longer, and no one spends time or thought on what is soon to be left behind.

Abundantly I have blessed you. Your gratitude for this is fitting. But there are far more wonderful things I am about to do for you, so keep your heart free and your mind stayed upon

Me. The Great Revelation is unfolding, and the ushering in of My Kingdom is at hand. I want to prepare you. I have truth to give you that is vital for this hour. You need to receive it now so you will not be perplexed.

It shall indeed be a dark hour for the world, and humanity will be enshrouded in a darkness such as in the days of the flood. This will be an even greater darkness, and there will be anguish and travail. But out of this will come a new age—of righteousness and of peace—and all creation will struggle in travail until it is brought forth.

But I am lifting My chosen ones even now into a realm of glory and revelation. Yes, I am bringing forth a special unique creation. It shall be as it was for Noah and Lot, the righteous remnant will be delivered out of destruction.

For judgment must fall upon sin and all ungodliness. Evil must be purged and put away. But I will always have a witness, and I will not forsake My people who put their trust in Me. The greater the judgment, the greater the deliverance; and the greater the darkness, the greater the glory. The greater the lie, the greater the Truth.

These are going to be glorious days for you, My chosen. (And this has been a mutual choosing. If the world would choose Me now, I would usher in My kingdom now, as in the days of Jesus' earthly ministry, when Israel had then the opportunity to accept her Messiah. Having rejected, judgment ensued. So it is today. Humanity has had nearly two thousand years to accept My grace and My forgiveness and salvation. Having rejected, doom is inevitable.)

This is the night of man's rebellion and disobedience. You are beginning to see the fulfillment of the second Psalm. But in this night, the door will be opened. It will be opened by the Bridegroom, and those who are watching and have maintained their lamps of witness will go in. Others will see and will desire to enter, but they will be too late.

See that your witness does not cease. Only as long as you have a full supply of My Spirit can the fire of testimony be kept alive. Those who hold darkened lamps could scarcely be unbe-lievers, for the lamp is My Word. My Word without My Spirit can produce no witness. The fire is the witness, and the fire comes never from the Word alone, but always from the Word and the oil of the Spirit. See that you do not lose the oil. When those who possess the oil have been taken away, where will you go to buy?

Be filled, My people, and be burning, for when I come I will come for the living, not for the dead; for the Living Witness I will preserve to carry the light over into the Kingdom Age.

WITH WINGED FEET

It is God who arms me with strength,
And makes my way perfect.
He makes my feet like the feet of deer,
And sets me on my high places.

PSALM 18:32

O My children, the time is short. Do not be like those who live for the pleasures of the moment, for all that is of the world is earthly. It will not endure, but will be like chaff carried away by the wind. I am aware of your needs and will provide in abundance, but it is for My glory and My honor, and I will have the praise.

You will tread lightly and not allow your feet to be ensnared in the net of undue concern for the things about you. They are Mine, just as all things are Mine, and you are Mine; and I am more interested in you than in things. Likewise, I want you to be occupied with Me rather than with My gifts. I will take care of both them and yourself. Is it not a small thing for Me to do?

Be alert to My voice. Let your ear not lose its keenness. Be devoted to Me with your whole heart, and put all that is around you into My keeping. For I have not many to whom I can speak as I have spoken to you. You will be My mouthpiece in places where there are no other voices to be heard.

You will magnify My Name in a dark corner. You will praise Me in a place where others extol men. You will show My love and reality to those who have not as yet experienced My nearness and fellowship in the way you have known Me.

I need you as a light to shine in dark places. I have not called you by some fickle whim. How will the message go out without a messenger? I have made you My messenger. You will go with winged feet. You will not allow your foot to be bogged down in the mire of earthly cares and riches.

You will discharge your duties with dispatch and will deal in wisdom with each responsibility; but your heart will rest in My hand. Your thoughts will return to Me as the needle to the pole and as the bird to its nest, season after season.

SOUNDING
OF THE TRUMPET

And everyone who has this hope in Him purifies himself,
just as He is pure.

1 JOHN 3:3

THE SECRET

There's a little word that changes
    Darkest skies to brightest blue;
There's a little word that brings the
    Sunlight bravely shining through.
Never mind the things around you;
    Never mind if others frown—
Lift your face to God and praise Him,
    And the blessings will come down!

Praise is mightier than an army
    With its banners all unfurled;
Praise will win the victory sooner
    Than all the powers of this world.
For the God who rules all things,
    And the God who longs to bless
Waits only till He hears you
    Your love to Him confess.

Beg Him not for any blessing;

    Tire Him not to spell your need.

This He knows e'er you speak it;

    Stay Him not to beg and plead.

Lift your face and sing it heav'nward,

    From the deeps within your soul;

Let His praises fill your being,

    Let the shout of rapture roll.

Ah! The rest will come quite easy—

    E'er you think, 'twill be done.

You will know PRAISE is the answer.

    You will find the vict'ry won.

Blessed, holy, wondrous Jesus,

    Heav'n in You to me is come!

DELIGHT YOURSELF IN ME

Delight yourself also in the LORD,
And He shall give you the desires of your heart.

PSALM 37:4

My child, do not be anxious concerning the growth of your soul. Leave it with Me. Have I not said that the lilies grow without taking thought of themselves? So must you, both in the natural and in the spiritual.

To be sure, there are conditions that must be met to insure healthy, normal development; however, these conditions are not created by anxiety, for it only works against them.

Be occupied with acquainting yourself with My character and My person. Revel in My fellowship. Your very association with Me, if sufficiently consistent, will bring about changes in your personality that will surprise you when discovered, just as you have so often experienced the joy of finding a new bloom on a cherished plant.

Turn your face toward Me, and leave to Me the responsibility of probing your soul. I am the Master Surgeon. I am skilled in all the cures of the soul as well as those of the body. Let Me care for your health.

Delight yourself in Me, and I will bring about what you desire to see in your character and personality. Feed upon My Word.

It is there you will come to a clearer understanding of My Person. Only as you know Me can you come to be more like Me.

In association with others, people take to themselves a measure of the mannerisms and ideologies of these other persons. So will it be for those who spend much time in My company.

Silently, and without conscious effort, you will be changed.

RELINQUISH YOUR WILL

And he who does not take his cross and follow after Me
is not worthy of Me.

MATTHEW 10:38

My heart is grieved by your independence. How would Joseph have felt if his father and family had remained at home, starving in the famine, when he had invited them to share the bountiful stores he had at his disposal and desired to share freely with them (see Genesis 45)?

Would he not have grieved far more deeply than over the unjust actions of his brothers who hated him? For to be rebuffed by a loved one causes pain not to be compared with the cruelties inflicted by an enemy. So your indifference and unresponsiveness to My call brings anguish to My soul, indeed, deeper grief than the crimes of the reprobate sinner. I have laid My rod upon the sinner, but I have laid My hand upon you.

And I have put My arm around you to draw you closer, but you have been impatient and irritable as though I sought to interfere with your liberty. I am able to give you greater liberty than you will ever find by seeking to be independent of Me. I seek not to interfere with your happiness, but I do require that you relinquish your will; for I cannot bless you as I desire until your will is yielded up and you accept Mine in exchange.

As you love Me, you accept My will as your own, and the caliber and extent of your love for Me may be accurately measured to the degree that you accept My will with a peaceful heart.

You can best sing "My Jesus, I Love You" when you can truly sing "Where He Leads Me, I Will Follow." . . . For whoever does not take up his cross daily to follow Me cannot be My disciple.

With the Strong Cords of My Faithfulness

O My child, I have loved you with an everlasting love.

With the strong cords of My faithfulness I have bound
 Myself to you.

Throughout all the days of your sojourn, I have been deeply
 concerned for you,
  never turning My attention from you.

Darkness may have pressed around your soul,
 but I was near at hand.

The night of affliction may obscure your vision,
 but the night and the day are both alike to Me.

When you pass through the waters, I am with you.

Whether you see Me or not, I am at your side.

Though at times you feel only aloneness, My hand is upon you,

My arm encircles you, and My heart is touched by your grief.

I suffered in all ways as you suffer, but you will never suffer
 as I suffered;

for I experienced one awful moment of separation
 from the Father;

while I have promised I will NEVER forsake you,
 and I will never leave you.

In Love I Chasten

Forty years You sustained them in the wilderness;
They lacked nothing.

NEHEMIAH 9:21

Behold, I am the Lord your God, the Eternal, the Almighty. The Alpha and the Omega, the Beginning and the Ending— the Great Unchanging One, yes, the Bright and Morning Star, that lights every one that comes into the world. And My light has not grown dim, but it increases more and more in its intensity as the day approaches: the great and terrible day of judgment when all men's hearts will be laid open to the scrutiny of the light of My truth.

My Truth abides forever, and no one will escape, for it will be as a flaming sword as it proceeds out of My mouth, and every mouth will be stopped. For in judgment I will come, to purge the world and to set up My Kingdom.

But I have sent My Holy Spirit into your hearts now that He might judge your hearts daily, so you may be accounted worthy to escape the day of wrath. For if you walk now in the light of My revealed truth and if you judge yourselves, you will not be judged at that coming day. And if you allow the searching eye of the Holy Spirit to find you out, then it will not be said to you, "Your sin will find you out" (Numbers 32:23).

Do not resist Me or harden your hearts. Do not provoke Me to use My chastening rod, for I love you. I would not drive you with a whip, nor bridle you with rein and bit to prevent you from plunging into error; but only let Me look into your eyes, and I will guide you in love and gentleness.

I take no pleasure in the affliction of My children. In love I chasten to prevent the deeper suffering involved should I allow you to go on in a path of evil. But My heart is glad when you walk close, with your hand in Mine, and we may talk over the plans for each day's journey and activities—work and pleasures—so that it becomes a happy way that we travel in mutual fellowship.

So pour out your praise to Me from a light heart. I will plan your path and we will go singing. No cloud will mar. No storm will break.

Praise God!—He not only knows the way that I take, but He will walk it with me, and I will find comfort in His companionship.

I Control the Winds

Guide our feet into the way of peace.

LUKE 1:79

My child, do not be dismayed by any calamity that befalls you. Your times are in My hand. Your way is open before Me, and I have all in My control. Never doubt My care. Never question My dealings.

You will know that I am leading you by the narrowness of the way. It is often a difficult and precipitous path; but I would assure you of My hand of protection. Do not think it strange that I bring you by this route, for I know there is a raucous crowd on the other road, and an abundance of places of entertainment and countless places to eat and to drink.

I am not taking you that way, because in the solitary and the steep and narrow way I will have the opportunity to deal with you and teach you; and you will be blessed and will learn to praise Me with uncontrollable joy.

I cannot produce saints and shape My character and image within you by allowing you full and unrestricted liberty. There can be nothing profitable for you in the matter of the growth of your soul if you go the way of abandon.

Put your life in My hands, and it will be for you a place of peace and of spiritual comfort. So long as you abide in this place, I will control the rains that fall upon you and the winds that blow. So long as you are in My hands, you are in a garrison the walls of which no enemy will scale.

$\mathcal{A}$LLOW ME ENTRANCE TO YOUR HEART

But we all, with unveiled face, beholding as in a mirror the glory
of the Lord, are being transformed into the same image
from glory to glory,
just as by the Spirit of the Lord.

2 CORINTHIANS 3:18

My people, be watchful and deep in prayer. I cannot mold you and shape you and perfect you unless you provide Me the opportunity to do so. I can only minister to the needs of your soul when you allow Me entrance to the hidden places of your heart.

You can set up a barrier against Me to prevent My entrance, and I will not interfere. Open wide your being to Me in the intimacy of prayer, and then, and only then, will I take the liberty to correct you and show you your faults.

I long to do this for you, because I desire to shape you into a closer resemblance to My divine nature. I would change your human frailties to My strength. I would take your resentments, and give you My grace. I would take your natural inclination to anger, and give you My unerring tendency to love and to forgive.

I am your God, and I rule the universe and keep it operating by My will. But to you I have given this most sacred thing: *your will*. I have given you so much freedom that you may even exercise that will against Me, if you choose to do so.

Yield to Me, and I will shape and form your soul to conform to My pattern of beauty and holiness. Much that is considered as holiness by human standards is distortion in My eyes. You are not prepared to judge your own life, nor to draw a pattern for piety.

Fix your heart upon Me, and as you behold My glory, you will be changed, and My own likeness will be formed within you.

COME INTO THE SECRET CHAMBERS OF COMMUNION

Pray to your Father who is in the secret place;
and your Father who sees in secret will reward you openly.

MATTHEW 6:6

O My beloved, My desire is for you. My heart longs after you. Do not grieve Me by your indifference. I would gather you; but you do not heed Me. I would embrace you and caress you; but you are impatient to be on your way. You cannot please Me thus.

I have called you to come into the secret chambers of solitary communion. They are dark; but the comfort of My Person is there. Out of darkness comes great treasure.

The dazzle and glitter of public life is attractive to the natural eye; but I would closet you away in the secret places of humility and discipline of soul, denying the things that pertain to the outward man in order to perfect the inner life and enrich your knowledge of Myself.

$\mathcal{I}$ Seek to Lift Your Load

Humble yourselves in the sight of the Lord,
and He will lift you up.

JAMES 4:10

Seek Me early; seek Me late; seek Me in the midst of the day.
You need Me in the early hours for direction and guidance and
for My blessing upon your heart. You need Me at the end of the
day to commit into My hands the day's happenings—both to
free yourself of the burdens and to give them over into My
hands so I may continue to work things out. And you need Me
more than ever in the busy hours, in the activities and responsibilities, so that I may give you My grace and My tranquility
and My wisdom.

I do not ask you to take time for Me with the intention of
placing a burden on you by requiring you to do so. Rather than
adding a requirement, I seek to lift your load. Rather than bur-
dening you with a devotional obligation, I desire to take the
tensions of life from you.

HEART-PURITY

Therefore submit to God. Resist the devil and he will flee from you.
Draw near to God and He will draw near to you.

JAMES 4:7–8

My children, it is not by grieving over your sins that they are forgiven. My forgiveness is in constant operation and you need only accept it. The cleansing of your heart and the restoration of your joy depends upon your full confession and willingness to repent and to renounce your sin. It is in this area that you need to exercise your soul toward the achievement of heart-purity, and until this work is accomplished (and maintained) you will not have inner peace.

This unrest and conflict you suffer is not caused by My attitude toward you but by your attitude toward yourself. You know that all is not well within. You would do well to seek My face in repentance until you have yielded to Me all that distresses you.

Much of what distresses you is truly sin, but you do not even recognize it as such. You are in truth plagued more by these unidentified enemies than by all the overt sins you have ever committed. For the overt sins are readily recognized and sorely grieved over, and for most of these forgiveness has already been received.

It is the little foxes that are spoiling the vine. Your vine has tender grapes. If you were bearing no fruit, you would not be so molested.

Rejoice in knowing that the enemy would not trouble you unless you were of some value to Me. It was not an evil man that the devil chose to try in Old Testament days, but one of whom it was written that he was perfect before his God (see Job 2:3).

No true saint who seeks to please Me escapes the onslaughts of the devil. He who commits himself to a life of prayer is a prime target. You need armor if you decide to go out to battle. In serving Me, you anger the enemy; he will not allow you to gain ground spiritually without hurling his poisoned arrows of doubts and accusations against you.

Resist him, as Scripture admonishes you. He is not courageous, but he is sly, and he is not easily discouraged. You can never escape his snare until you recognize his activities and strike at the source.

Do not attack your discouragement, but resist the one who would burden you with it. Do not doubt My forgiveness, but close your ears to the accuser.

Your Life Is As a Weaving

Let the peace of God rule in your hearts.

COLOSSIANS 3:15

My child, your life is as a weaving. Beauty will not come to you by joy alone. Life may be tortuous at times and the pathway rough. From fabrics of lovely silk and from cords of rougher materials, I fashion what pleases Me. You may never know why certain experiences come. It is enough that My hand brings them all.

My grace is not limited by sorrow and difficulty. Indeed, it shines like a strand of gold mixed in with the black of grief. My hand moves with infinite love, and I am creating a pattern of intricate beauty.

Never be dismayed. The end will bring rejoicing for both yourself and Me. For you are My workmanship, created in Christ, even in His mind before the worlds existed.

Doubt not, for My will *shall be* done.

He took away the stain of sin
And made me clean and pure within;
He took away the strain of care
And now I find peace everywhere.

I WAIT FOR YOU

It is the voice of my beloved!
He knocks, saying,
"Open for me, my sister, my love. . . ."

SONG OF SOLOMON 5:2

Behold, with great love have I chosen you and made you Mine. My heart is drawn toward you, and I would minister to you.

I wait for you to turn from everything else to Me alone. I want you to give Me all of yourself. I want the real you. The more you can bring to Me of your true self, the more I can give to you of My true self.

If you come to Me with any kind of cloak over your soul, to this extent only you hinder Me from fully opening My heart to you. I am neither disturbed by imperfections nor impressed with piety. People look upon the outward, but I am only concerned with the heart; for I know that whenever I can occupy the heart, all will be working toward perfection in the outer person.

And so I bypass the outer person temporarily, and when I come to you, I come via the very citadel of your soul—not as an intruder from the outside.

It is as though a guest came to a home and entered the inner sanctum, rather than coming by way of the outer gate. He would be unconcerned about the gate or the garden or the exterior of the house. I come to you via My Holy Spirit from depths within your being that you have never plumbed, from chambers within your soul your eyes have never seen. Rooms of darkness. Not dark because of sin, necessarily, as you think of sin; but dark because they have been kept closed.

Indeed, only I have the key to open them. I not only have the power to open them, but the wisdom and the love; and I never confront you with anything without giving you the grace to meet the challenge.

*E*NTER THE FLOW

Take My yoke upon you and learn from Me,
for I am gentle and lowly in heart,
and you will find rest for your souls.

MATTHEW 11:29

O My child, My child, I love you. I need you. I need you because I love you. I call you through the trees. In the soughing of the pines, it is My voice speaking. I call you in the wind. In the breaking of the waves, it is My voice you hear. In the tumbling waters of the brook, it is I, calling, ever calling.

Go from your house with an open ear. Do not walk in a garden with inattentive soul. Do not pluck a flower without feeling your heart throb.

Learning, knowing, working, these all have their place. But these are not the core of life, for living at its center is loving; anything else is not life. Work becomes the fabric from which we weave life only when love holds the threads. Knowledge enriches life to the degree that love controls the thinking. Pleasure becomes the path to the far country if true love has been left behind in pursuit of false values.

Learn to love Me and to love Me well. Let the voice within you answer the voice without. Be at one with the trees, with the waves, with the flowing brook. Grow upward, as trees, and seek My face. Dwell deep, as the lake, and know My fullness and quiet. And move ever, always, determinedly onward as the brook does; and keep the outflow of your life ever in motion.

For in My speaking, you will gain insight. In My stillness, you will gain poise; and joining with Me in the flow, you will experience the progressive life. Yes, only as life is progressive is it life at all. Movement indicates life. Movement safeguards life. Movement promulgates life. Movement gives purpose to life—yes, beauty.

It is the flowing lines of the sculptor's work that spell success. It is the flowing movement of the musical score that transforms mere notes to true song. It is the ministries of mother to child, either physical or spiritual, that contribute to the formation of the new personality and character. It is in the fulfillment of the joint responsibilities and services between husband and wife that love is nurtured and fulfillment experienced.

It is love *being* and love *doing*. Yes, it is love loving. Otherwise love is concept, not reality. It is the believer worshiping—otherwise it is empty religion, with all spiritual creativity lost, and if not found in time, destroyed.

So the trees would say to you, *Speak*. Speak to Me, speak of Me—for I am always speaking.

And the lake would say to you, *Be still*. Be still before Me in communion, and be still at times even in the company of others, so you may enjoy the lesson of the lake in mutual fellowship.

And *Move*. Find the channel of creativity within your soul. I have made no one without it. Some have choked it with indifference; others have despised it in rebellion; others have ignored it in foolishness; others have twisted it in bitterness. But I stand ready to come to the assistance of any man or woman who sincerely endeavors to find this channel, to remove debris, to repair damage or straighten the course, and most of all to enter the flow.

It is the flow of divine life. Dam it off by self-centeredness and it becomes a dead sea. Labor, learn, attempt to live apart from its power and impetus, and all is ultimately weariness of body, frustration of soul, disappointment of heart, and failure in purpose.

Come to Me, all you who labor and are heavy laden; enter the stream of My life and you will find rest, you will find power, you will find overflowing joy, you will discover with delight that you have truly become partaker of My life, co-laborer in My Father's work, and recipient of inestimable rewards.

_I_ MAKE NO PROVISION FOR THE LAGGARD

Righteousness will go before Him,
And shall make His footsteps our pathway.

PSALM 85:13

I am in the midst of you, My children. You have heard My voice and have known that I have been ministering to you. You have not followed the voice of a stranger nor sought out strange paths. For this reason have I set My love upon you. I have put My arm around you, and with My wings have I sheltered you. You are the object of My special attention, and you have received My special care.

I have given you of My best because you have loved Me. I have drawn you into My banquet hall because you hungered and thirsted after the things of God. Because you have longed for righteousness and true holiness, I sought you out to instruct you and teach you in My laws and in My ways. I will indeed bring you to a higher realm of experience and revelation because there is a quest in your soul after Truth.

The Word is truly near you, even in your heart. Listen to the voice of My Spirit within. It will never fail. It will never be silent. It will never mock your cry. Your hours of meditation will be rich in the treasures of your God, and His light will guide you.

It is no futile path in which I am leading you. It will be laden with blessing and filled with surprises. Never be hesitant to follow. If you lag behind, you may find My footprints have become cold because I have gone on too far ahead. I charge you to keep pace with Me. I will not gauge My steps too wide for you to follow. I will measure them to your ability, but I make no provision for the laggard.

Follow close, and your reward will be blessed.

The Solitary Relationship

When You said, "Seek My face,"
My heart said to You, "Your face, LORD,
I will seek."

PSALM 27:8

Praise Me out of the fullness of your heart. Out of the depths of your soul let your songs arise. For I have dealt bountifully with you; I have blessed you in abundance and have multiplied your joys. I have set you in a safe place; I made you to dwell in the mountain of My grace; I have covered you with My mercies. Blessed be My Name, for I will surround you with My presence and satisfy your heart with My love.

Never be dismayed, nor allow any anxiety to find a nesting place in your thoughts. For you are Mine, and My hand will protect you. I will allow no evil to come to you.

You are My possession. I will brook no rivalry. Rebuke the enemy and he will flee from you. Count upon My care: I cannot fail. He that keeps his confidence in Me will never be disappointed.

This is a solitary walk. This abiding place in Me is completely removed from the multitude; it is a place to be shared with no other—not even your dearest friend. This knowing Me in secret is an experience alien to the world. This union with

Me is the source of your life, of your strength, of your health and vitality. Nothing can substitute.

Prayer is good, but prayer cannot substitute for solitary communion. Fellowship is good, but it is not the source of Life. Life is in Me, and I can give it to you only in the solitary relationship. Seek that place in Me where no other can intrude. You will find Me there, and in finding Me, you will discover all other lacks fulfilled; for in Me there is abundant Life, and with Me there are only joys, forever.

$\mathcal{B}$ E VIGILANT

My people, lift up your voice and weep aloud.

Yes, let your cry be heard in the night.

In the stillness, rouse the sleeping.

Say to My people, Get up, shake yourself from slumber.

Lay aside your garments of sleep.

Gird yourself and put sandals on your feet.

Make haste.

Yes, flee to the rock of refuge lest in your drowsiness,

sleeping past the hour, you waken at last

to find yourself ensnared in the net of the enemy.

For the powers of darkness are around you on every side.

He does not rest in his scheming and plotting.

For he desires with an unholy, fiendish delight

and with bitter, deliberate design,

to destroy the godly and to break down the building

of God.

But I have built My Church, and founded it upon the Rock,

and the very gates of hell shall not prevail against it.

I would not have you be unaware of his devices;

but having calculated the strength of the opposing force you

    will see your need for greater power—

        so you will not be overcome.

For My power is available to you.

Yes, I Myself will fight for you if you put your trust in Me.

        Only be vigilant.

    For those who stumble, stumble in the darkness,

    and those who slumber do so in the night.

        Do not be overtaken.

Fix your eyes upon the Sun of Righteousness

    and He shall cause you to walk in a path of light.

According to My Eternal Purposes

Hold fast, for I am with you:
Stand still, for I am your God.
Be quiet before Me,
For I have arranged all things for you according to My
good will,
yes, according to My eternal purposes.

For I have purposes and plans and desires
which reach far beyond your present view.
You see only the immediate situation,
but My thoughts for you and My planning
for you embrace eternity.
Yes, you are in My hand.
Rest there, and leave all else to Me.

THESE ARE DAYS OF THE MOVING OF MY SPIRIT

"Behold, the days are coming," says the Lord GOD,
"That I will send a famine on the land,
Not a famine of bread,
Nor a thirst for water,
But of hearing the words of the LORD."

AMOS 8:11

Be alert. Be on guard. Give no offense either to the receptive or the unreceptive, for this changes from day to day, and the unconcerned today may be the most concerned tomorrow, and vice versa. Do not attempt to make a judgment as to who is hungry for more of God. At any moment an appetite long dormant may be aroused, and the longer it has been dormant, the more voracious it will be.

Give My Word—My Word alone will whet the appetite. Give them a drink. The water will awaken new thirst. You will say, "How will I be able to satisfy so great a demand?" These are the days of the moving of My Spirit; will you resist if I wish to make you My aqueduct?

Stay clear—allow no constriction nor obstruction, and do not be stingy. Growth will spring forth wherever the waters reach.

GIVE NO SUBSTITUTES

Did the word of God come originally from you?
Or was it you only that it reached?

1 CORINTHIANS 14:36

My people are hungering for My Word, and when you are gathered together, I would that you feed them.

Give no inedible substitutes. Give the lovely bread of the words of Jesus. Spread a feast, and enjoy the delicious and rich meats of divine truth.

Why should you hunger when plenty is at hand? And why should you be deprived of spiritual nourishment when a table is spread before you?

Some of the foods may be strange to you. Despise nothing that I offer you. You need it, or else I would not provide it. Partake of it, even if it is strange to your taste. You will soon come to relish it with delight, and even more so because it is a new experience for you.

Keep your mind open; how else can you grow? Fear no deception nor poison. So long as you seek Me, you will be rewarded in finding Me. What you *seek*, you will *find*.

You will not seek bread and find a stone. You will not seek fish and find a scorpion. You need have no fear except the fear of a misdirected quest. Let My Holy Spirit reign in the desires of your heart, and you shall be guarded from unworthy motives. Let Me keep your motives free of selfish lusts, channeled into the paths of righteousness.

Open your eyes to all I show you; open your mouth wide and let Me fill it as I have promised to do.

Your eyes will be filled with wonder and your mouth with good things. My words will come *to* you, and My truth will come *forth* from you.

STAY BENEATH MY WING

When you pass through the waters, I will be with you;
And through the rivers, they shall not overflow you.
When you walk through the fire, you shall not be burned,
Nor shall the flame scorch you.

ISAIAH 43:2

My people: Will I create, and will I not have it in My power to destroy? Is it not written that the potter breaks one vessel that He may shape a new one (see Jeremiah 18:4)? Will I not do likewise? Yes, I will bring My will to pass, and man will know that his will is like a broken straw when pitted against the Almighty.

But My people will know the protection of their God. Because their heart is stayed upon Jehovah, I will keep them in My pavilion and shelter them until the calamity passes.

If I removed you from the scene, you would have no testimony of My miraculous delivering power. Stay beneath My wings, and I will make you a tower of strength to which the fearful may run and find safety.

BREAD UPON THE WATERS

Cast your bread upon the waters,
For you will find it after many days.

ECCLESIASTES 11:1

Do not be afraid to follow Me, nor draw back in doubt. I will provide all that you lack, and I will pave the way for you with My bounty.

You are not treading alone. There are many with you on the same road. It is the road of faith and trust, and you will have sweet fellowship, for there are others who will join you in this walk.

You will rejoice with exceeding joy, and your joy shall be shared by angels. They walk beside you and guard your way.

Never limit Me. I will take you through, though cliffs should rise before you. There will always be a provision, and in My mercy I will see that you find it.

Be humble and be patient. I am nearer to you than you think, and I will do more than you expect. I work in every heart to bring conformity to My Word. You only need give it. I will do the subsequent work, for My Word is living and powerful. It will not come to failure. It will accomplish My purpose, though My purpose may be entirely hidden from you.

The Master Artist

Then God saw everything that He had made,
and indeed it was very good.

GENESIS 1:31

Set your gaze toward heaven. Your eyes will behold My glory.

I have brought you through the testing time, and My heart rejoices over you. You see but a part of the picture, but I see the design in its completion. You cannot know what is in My mind and what I am creating with the materials of your life.

Only yield yourself into My hands. You need not make your own plans, for I am in control, and you would bring disaster by interference, just as the untrained use of the brush by a helpful child would ruin the canvas of the master artist.

So rest your soul, knowing that I have been at work in ways you have least suspected; for the picture in your thinking and the work I was engaged in were entirely different.

I make no idle strokes. What I do is never haphazard. I am never merely mixing colors out of casual curiosity. My every move is one of vital creativity, and every stroke is part of the whole.

Never be dismayed by apparent incongruity. Never be alarmed by a sudden dash of color seemingly out of context. Say only to your questioning heart, "It is the Infinite wielding

His brush; I know He does all things well."

And in all that I do with a free hand, without interference, I can stand back and view the work and say, "It is good."

I AM BRINGING SONS INTO GLORY

We should no longer be children, tossed to and fro
and carried about with every wind of doctrine, by the trickery of men,
in the cunning craftiness of deceitful plotting,
but, speaking the truth in love, may grow up in all things
into Him who is the head—Christ.

EPHESIANS 4:14-15

My people are precious to Me. No evil shall befall them without My knowledge. My grace I lavish upon them to conform them to My image. My energies I give for their nurture and development.

I have not simply brought forth children, but am bringing sons into glory. I have rejoiced in their birth, but rejoice more deeply in their maturity.

Be babies no longer, but grow. Fed by the Word of God and

succored by prayer, let your development into full stature be accomplished.

My hand is upon you. Draw close. There may be times when I must wield the rod of correction, but this is for your ultimate good.

Blessing will be held back and growth retarded if you resist My discipline.

SHOUT THE VICTORY

Whatever is born of God overcomes the world.
And this is the victory that has overcome the world—our faith.

My people shall be like an army. They shall move at My command, and they shall see the victory. I will not send them into an empty valley. I send them against an onrushing foe, bent on destruction and armed to the teeth with deadly weapons. They will overcome them, for I will be their strength, and I will make the strength of one to be as the strength of ten. I go before and carry the banner.

Shout the victory. Your God will respond. I will even put to flight the armies of the enemy by the sound of My response.

Peace will come as a quiet morning and as the stillness of dew.

As the Sounding of the Trumpet

The world has hated them because they are not of the world,
just as I am not of the world.

JOHN 17:14

Be patient, My beloved, for the coming of the Lord is at hand. Establish your hearts in Me, and be faithful. The Kingdom is at hand, and will I not make preparation? I do not have My prophets simply as demonstrations of the miraculous; I have them for the purpose of communicating My message to My people.

Never has it been more important that they hear Me. It is as vital at this hour as the contact between an army and their commander. You dare not risk being cut off. You need direction as never before. You also need to know the position and strategy of the opponent. This is a cumulative climax. Past battles will be like child's play by comparison. This is an all-out offensive I am about to launch. Gird up your loins. Gather up the supplies. Lay aside every hindrance.

My Word will go forth as the sounding of the trumpet. It will be clear and distinct. It will not waver. Many will hear and be alerted; yes, those who live in the Spirit will hear, but the dead will go on about their work as deaf men. No sign will be given to them except the sign of My people being gathered out. The hard of heart, the callous in spirit will misinterpret and condemn. They will not see My hand, for it will be hidden from them. For if they knew the truth they would follow. But I will not allow this, for it is better that you be misunderstood than joined by those whose hearts are unchanged and unprepared.

For My people are a people chosen by Me. See that you give no heed to the cries of scorn. Close your ears to all who would detain you. Cover your head and run as one who runs for his life. For truly not your life only, but the lives of your children are at stake. Be as deaf to others as they are deaf to Me.

Surely I am doing a work of righteousness, even in the earth. For I say to you, you are not of the world, even though you are in the world. I will wash your feet and cleanse you from the defilement of the way. I will fit you to walk in a path of holiness. I will put away false doctrine, and you shall hear truth. You shall eat the good of the land. You shall flourish and be made fruitful.

Because you have sought Me, I will bless you; I will stand in your midst. I will even joy over you with singing.

You Will Come Forth as Gold

You are my portion, O LORD;
I have said that I would keep Your words.
I entreated Your favor with my whole heart;
Be merciful to me according to Your word.

PSALM 119:57–58

I know the way that you take, and when you come forth, you will come forth as gold, yes, as pure gold, having been tried in the fire. For My eye is upon you in loving watchfulness, and My ear is open to your cry.

Never be overcharged with anxiety. I am your burden-bearer. Never be anxious for the morrow, for on the morrow I will be your sure supply. Praise Me *now,* and let your confidence in Me be manifest. So will the faith of others be encouraged, for your life is a witness to many.

The Lord is your portion: He shall keep you in peace. Because you have made the Most High your abiding place, He shall deliver you in trouble. He shall bless you and reward you, and reveal to you the greatness of His salvation.

$\mathcal{I}$ SHALL COME SINGING

Be ready, for the Son of Man is coming at an hour you do not expect.

LUKE 12:40

My children, be silent before Me that I may speak to you. I will lift up My voice as the sound of a trumpet—I will speak clearly to you, for the hour is at hand.

Be obedient, and raise your standards of discipline and dedication to a higher level. For My face is set toward My imminent return to earth. I wait only the release from the Father's hand. I long to come, and to be united with My chosen ones; but the Father holds the times in His own power.

And I say to you, though I am ready and longing to come to you, yes, I would have rejoiced to have come much sooner, I say to you, you are not yet ready. I have wooed you and I have warned you. You have spurned My entreaties, and you have fought against the restraints of the Spirit.

Break through your religious curtain, and behold Me in My glory. Keep your vision filled with Me. Keep your life in tune and your worship in mutual harmony.

For I will come singing, and what will you be if you are in discord?

Expect the Unexpected

Then Philip went down to the city of Samaria
and preached Christ to them.
And the multitudes with one accord heeded the things spoken by Philip,
hearing and seeing the miracles which he did.

ACTS 8:5–6

O My child, let Me speak to you, and let My Spirit direct your life. I may lead you in unexpected ways, and ask things of you that are startling, but I will never guide you amiss.

Across your path will fall the shadow of My hand, and wherever I direct you, there will you see My power at work, and your ministry will glorify Me.

Do not walk according to your natural reasoning, but obey the promptings of the Spirit, and be obedient to My voice.

I need those who will be completely flexible in this way, because a multitude of souls are searching for Me, and would never come into contact with Me in a personal way through the channels of the organized church.

You shall go as Philip went—at the direction of the Spirit—into the places that are out of the way, and bring light on My Word to those who are in need.

Stay in an attitude of prayer and faith, and I will do all the rest.

ETERNAL DESTINY OF THE PRESENT MOMENT

Be an example to the believers in word,
in conduct, in love, in spirit, in faith, in purity.

1 TIMOTHY 4:12

O My child, it is not appointed to you to know the future, nor to be able to discern beforehand My exact plans. It is enough that we should walk together in love and trust. No doubts need mar your peace, nor anxieties cloud your brow. Rest in the knowledge that My ways are perfect and My grace is all-sufficient. You will find My help is adequate, no matter what may befall you.

Let no one say to you, "This will be, or that will surely come to pass." Live, rather, in the awareness of the eternal destiny of the present moment. To be unduly occupied with matters of the future is to your own disadvantage. So much is waiting to be done now.

It is written: "Till I come, give attention to reading, to exhortation, to doctrine" (1 Timothy 4:13). Live according to this injunction. Your life is in My hands. I can only use what is available to Me at the moment. Others need guidance and help with their present problems. Minister in the realm of the here and now, and you will have much fruit in the day of reaping.

SCRIPTURE REFERENCE INDEX

OTHER BOOKS
BY FRANCES J. ROBERTS

Come Away My Beloved
Original Edition
ISBN 0-932814-02-6

Dialogues with God
ISBN 0-932814-08-5

Make Haste My Beloved
ISBN 0-932814-26-3

On the High Road of Surrender
ISBN 0-932814-15-8

Progress of Another Pilgrim
ISBN 0-932814-11-5

Total Love
ISBN 0-932814-33-6

Available wherever books are sold.